Democratization in Confucian East Asia

Democratization in Confucian East Asia

Citizen Politics in China, Japan, Singapore, South Korea, Taiwan, and Vietnam

Zhengxu Wang

CAMBRIA
PRESS

Youngstown, New York

Library of Congress Cataloging-in-Publication Data

Wang, Zhengxu.
Democratization in confucian East Asia : citizen politics in China, Japan, Singapore, South Korea, Taiwan, and Vietnam / Zhengxu Wang.
p. cm.
Includes bibliographical references and index.
ISBN 978-1-934043-99-8 (alk. paper)
1. Democratization—East Asia. 2. Social values—East Asia. 3. East Asia—Economic conditions. I. Title.

JQ1499.A91W36 2007
320.95—dc22

2007040085

民为贵，社稷次之，君为轻。

— «孟子 · 尽心下»

People are the most important element. The state is the second. The ruler is the least important.

—Mencius (*Meng Tzu*), 391–289 BC

Table of Contents

List of Tables

List of Figures

Acknowledgments

First, I want to thank the academic advisors for my doctoral studies at the University of Michigan, Professor Ronald Inglehart and Professor Marvin Peterson, both of whom served as models of scholarly life for me. They offered encouragement and guidance—the best things a student can ever wish for. Ron opened the door for me to the study of democratization and supported my studies, especially my dissertation effort. Marv always served as a source of knowledge, confidence, and stimulation. From him I learned how to live an academic life. Without their continuous and passionate encouragement and insightful advice, this project would not have been possible. Professor Janet Lawrence, Professor Mary Gallagher, and Professor Mark Tessler of the University of Michigan also played important roles in the making of this study. I want to thank especially Professor Janet Lawrence of the Center for the Studies of Higher and

Postsecondary Education (CSHPE) for her care and assistance during my years in Ann Arbor.

On my path to becoming a member in academia, many people offered important support. I thank Professor Ellis Joffe for his early guidance when I first entered the China studies field. Professor Eric Dey and Professor Sylvia Hurtado offered me important financial support in graduate school. At the National University of Singapore, Professor Wang Gungwu, Professor John Wong, Professor Dali Yang, Professor Ern Ser Tan provided great support. Professor Doh Shin always followed my growth. Professor Christian Welzel offered his invaluable advice. Ms. Ying Yang provided important editorial assistance. Thanks also to Ms. Toni Tan and staff at Cambria Press for their patience and assistance.

***

It is normal practice to dedicate a book to someone special to the author. Should this book be dedicated to anyone, it would be to my parents. I am ever thankful for their faith in my course and their patience in my effort. Nevertheless, I am not making such a dedication—I know they will be happy with anything I do. I take this step because I hope my work, starting with this book, will serve a higher purpose.

Most educated Chinese know the name Qian Zhongshu (钱钟书), and many have read his novel *Wei Cheng* (围城*Fortress Besieged)* or have seen its TV version. This masterful book, characteristically, does *not* have a dedication page. The author has a point. Dedication, he says, is like knives released without ever leaving the magician's hands. It is like a politician saying he is offering his life to his nation or a military strongman saying he is returning the reins of the government to the people. Despite all the fine words of a dedication, he says, the book remains the author's own. So, he says, why bother with such "ingenious disingenuousness"?*

Qian Zhongshu is one of the Western-influenced Chinese whose lives had in various ways intertwined with that of 20th-century China. Among them are men and women of ideas and letters: Chen Yinke (陈寅恪), Wang Guowei (王国维), Liang Qichao (梁启超), Cai Yuanpei (蔡元培), Li Dazhao (李大钊), Yang Jiang (杨绛), Lu Xun (鲁迅), Yan Fu (严复), Hu Shi (胡适), Cao Yu (曹禺), and Lao She (老舍); men and women of science and social science: Zhan Tianyou (詹天佑), Li Siguang (李四光), Qian Xuesen (钱学森), Feng Youlan (冯友兰), Ji Xianlin (季羡林), and Fei Xiaotong (费孝通); and men and women of action: Liang Shuming (梁漱溟), Chen Duxiu (陈独秀), He Xiangning (何香凝), Cai Chang (蔡畅), and Zhang Shizhao (章世钊). To the last group I add Zhou Enlai (周恩来) and Deng Xiaoping (邓小平). By following the practice of Qian Zhongshu in omitting a dedication, I pay tribute to these great individuals, the most shining ones China has had.

* Translation credit: Keanne Kelly and Nathan Mao.

Democratization in Confucian East Asia

Part I

Introduction

CHAPTER 1

DEMOCRATIZATION IN MODERNIZING SOCIETIES

Uncertainty hovers over the prospect of democracy in East Asia as we enter the 21st century. On the one hand, democracy remains stable in Japan, despite the country's sluggish economy, while democracies in South Korea, Taiwan, and Mongolia, established in the 1990s, struggle toward maturation in their own ways. On the other hand, democracy seems unlikely for many of the region's societies. North Korea and Myanmar claim two of the most repressive regimes in the world. Despite sustained economic growth for more than 2 decades, democratization still seems out of reach in China. Similarly, in Singapore, Vietnam, and Laos, strong one-party regimes rule steadfastly. In 2006, a coup in Thailand, never a stable democracy, once again wrestled the country to military rule. Between these two ends are the unstable or pseudo democracies of the Philippines,

Indonesia, Cambodia, and Malaysia. Measured by stricter standards, of the 17 total polities in this region, only four qualify as democracies, amounting to less than one in four.[1] Against this backdrop, one might ask, will East Asia see more countries become democratic? Will the existing democracies become better democracies?

This book looks at how economic growth and social modernization in East Asia have resulted in a growing prodemocratic public and how these increasingly prodemocratic citizens prepare solid foundations for democracy while demanding more democratic institutions. I focus this study on East Asia's six Confucian societies: Japan, South Korea, China, Taiwan, Vietnam, and Singapore. These societies provide an excellent group for examining the relationships between economic development, value changes, and democratic politics. Several conditions make the study of these societies a near optimal and natural experiment. First, these societies share a common Confucian cultural heritage. This provides an almost ideal pool of cases for comparative political cultural studies: these societies' similar heritage in the Confucian belief system enables us to insulate variables that may have caused value differences. Second, at the end of World War II these countries shared similar economic development levels, with the exception of Japan. And third, since then, speedy economic development has occurred in each of these societies, but at very different times. The different time points at which economic developments took off in different societies enable us to examine whether economic development does lead to changes in a society's value system.

This book argues that as a result of economic development and social changes, these East Asian societies have seen a steady growth of prodemocratic attitudes among their publics. Largely following economic acceleration of each individual society, such value changes started in Japan during the 1930s; in the newly industrialized countries of South Korea, Taiwan, and Singapore during the 1950s and 1960s; in China during the 1980s; and in Vietnam in the 1990s. These prodemocratic attitudes translated into pressures on the ruling elites, who then had to introduce political liberalization and institutional reforms. In Japan, such rising public pressures led to reform in democratic institutions, resulting in a higher quality of democracy. In South Korea and Taiwan, the process grew and evolved through the 1980s and 1990s, amounting to a thorough transition from authoritarianism to democracy. In China, public pressure for political openness started to simmer in the late 1980s, with much political liberalization and relaxation taking place. Similar patterns have arisen in Vietnam, following its economic liberalization starting in the 1990s. In general, democratization in East Asia likely will follow the patterns manifested in South Korea and Taiwan: democratization will take place following a rise in people's prodemocratic values caused by a significant period of economic development and social modernization.

This book focuses on China, as well. To a large extent, democracy in East Asia depends on whether China will become a stable democracy. Without China's becoming a democracy, the democratization of its smaller neighbors such as North Korea, Vietnam, Laos, Cambodia, and Myanmar will stall or remain unlikely, while democracy in Taiwan and even in South Korea will suffer negative consequences. Leaving such regional implications aside, China is itself important for the study of democracy.

Until the country with the world's largest population and fourth largest economy (on the way to becoming the second largest) becomes a democracy, the assertion that democracy represents a universal value remains contestable.

VALUE AND DEMOCRACY IN EAST ASIA

Through the years, many have argued that liberal democracy cannot work in East Asia as a form of government. On the one hand, Western scholars argue that Confucian ethics and political philosophy contain many antidemocratic principles (Huntington, 1991). For example, Lucian Pye considers Chinese political culture totally undemocratic (Pye, 1968). Indeed, from time to time, Confucianism, Buddhism, and Taoism receive criticism for being nondemocratic. If citizens believe in nondemocratic values, some critics ask, how can a society build democracy? But on the other hand, some Asian leaders argue that the West's highly divisive and individualistic democracy goes against the Asian people's ideal of good government and good society—the "Asian Values" argument (Zabaria, 1994). Hence, it is not that Asian values are undemocratic, it is that democracy does not complement Asian values.

As the ideological foundation for traditional Chinese hierarchical social and political system, Confucianism does contain elements stressing order, hierarchy, and respect for authority. But so does every other kind of ideology that formed the basis of preindustrial social orders. On the other hand, Confucianism and other Asian philosophical traditions also offer ideas, ideals, and elements of a good society and good government, and many of these are humanistic and democratic (Chan, 1998; Tu,

2000b). For this reason, many argue that a Confucian heritage dovetails perfectly with modernity (Tu, 2000a), and Confucian culture is in fact "a-democratic" (Hua, 2000).

This book leaves aside the "Asian Values" debate. I assert, as many others do, that modernization will produce values that challenge authority and embrace democratic principles (Heng, 1997). Recent scholarship in human development and democracy convincingly argues that aspirations to liberty and democracy lie latent in every human being. Once socioeconomic conditions allow people to take survival for granted, they show a predisposition for liberty and democratic social and political life. In other words, human desires for liberty, freedom, and emancipation naturally arise once industrialization and economic development take off (Welzel, Inglehart, & Klinngamen, 2003). Hence, regardless of the ideology or culture that exists in an agrarian society, it will give way to a set of proliberty, proequality, proemancipation, and prodemocracy values. This set of values I call *self-expression values.* As economic development continues, the strength of self-expression values of a society also grows. An increasingly self-expression-oriented citizenry will demand political openness, which results in more democratic government. Scholars have recently dubbed this a human development perspective of democratization (Inglehart & Welzel, 2005).

Plan of the Book

This book answers the question: why and how will social and economic developments lead to a more democratic East Asia? I argue that economic growth and social changes in East Asia will give rise to prodemocratic self-expression values. With stronger self-expression values, citizens in these societies will become more assertive in demanding political changes, and they will also become more active in civil society. In both ways, they contribute to long-term democratization of these societies.

Part I contains two introductory chapters. In chapter 2, I lay out a framework for understanding the process of democratization. This framework puts citizens at the center of political changes in modernizing societies. Economic and social modernization result in self-expression-oriented citizens, who in turn drive political changes by building a strong civil society and demanding political openness from the government. Chapter 3 reviews scholarly works on the relationship between citizen values and democracy, focusing on the human development theory of democratization and explaining the argument of how self-expression values lead to more democratic governments around the world.

Chapters 4 and 5 make up Part II, which examines the rise of self-expression values in the six societies in Confucian Asia. They present empirical evidence of how economic development and social modernization results in stronger self-expression values in these societies. Chapter 4 looks at economic and social modernization as a holistic process, while chapter 5 looks at education as one element within broader economic and social development.

Part III of the book examines the political consequences of self-expression values. Chapters 6 through 8 present empirical evidence for how self-expression values give rise to democratic citizenship in these societies. In chapter 6, I demonstrate that strong self-expression values lead to high protest propensity.

That is, people with stronger self-expression values will more likely challenge government authorities through petitions and protests. In chapter 7, I demonstrate that strong self-expression values lead to more active civic participation: citizens with stronger self-expression values are more actively involved in civil society groups. Chapter 8 presents yet another linkage between self-expression values and challenge to government: political trust. Citizens with stronger self-expression values are more likely to be critical citizens: more likely to distrust government, they are hence more inclined to hold the government accountable.

In the concluding Part IV, chapter 9 links empirical findings with existing theories about value change and democracy. Specifically, is a prodemocratic culture forming in China? Is the pressure on the regime to introduce democratic changes building? How optimistic can we be about democratization in China in the upcoming years? I argue that given the existing evidence, it is reasonable to believe that by around 2020, China will likely see major institutional changes toward democratization, such as a free press and free elections. Chapter 10 wraps up the whole book.

Comparative Data

World Values Survey (WVS), a cross-national attitudinal survey, started in 1981, has been conducted around the world in four waves. The First Wave covered about two dozen countries largely concentrated in Western Europe, with only two East Asian countries (Japan and Korea) included. By the time the Fourth Wave was finished in 2001–2002, the survey had covered more than 60 societies and over 80% of the world's population, generating a huge amount of research. The survey asks respondents' opinions on family, work, society, government, religion, and personal life. Earlier research on such data has identified significant and coherent patterns of value change in different societies (Inglehart, 1997).

Sample Size

For the countries of interest in my study, WVS contains four waves of data from Japan and South Korea (1980, 1990, 1995, & 2000), three waves of data from China (1990, 1995, & 2000), and one wave of data from Taiwan (1995), Vietnam (2001), and Singapore (2002). Table 1.1 shows the sample sizes of each wave of WVS in the countries included in the current study.

The WVS headquarters coordinates this project using a unified survey questionnaire and a representative country sample.

Table 1.1. Sample size for selected countries.

Year	*1981*	*1990*	*1995–1996*	*2000–2001*	*Total*
Countries					
China		1,000	1,500	1,000	3,500
Taiwan			1,452		1,452
South Korea	970	1,251	1,249	1,200	4,670
Japan	1,204	1,011	1,054	1,362	4,631
Vietnam				1,500	1,500
Singapore				1,500	1,500
Total	2,174	3,262	5,255	6,562	17,253

Source. WVS.

Data collection in each society was directed by a country-specific principal investigator or a team of principal investigators. This study will largely rely on the four waves of survey data from the six countries mentioned earlier. Most of the comparative research will concentrate on the Fourth-Wave data, as it is the most recent and covers the largest number of surveyed societies. To benefit from the largest cross-national data set on human values, from time to time, the data of other WVS countries will also be included in the analysis.

NOTE

1. That is, only Japan, South Korea, Mongolia, and Taiwan are qualified democracies. Using more relaxed criteria, Freedom House rates the Philippines, Indonesia, and East Timor as democracies as well. See *Freedom in the World,* 2006 (Freedom House).

CHAPTER 2

BRINGING PEOPLE BACK IN

Two major arguments have long dominated the study of democratization: a structural argument and an actor-centered argument. The structural argument looks at socioeconomic conditions deemed favorable for the rise of democracy. Most notably, modernization theorists argue that socioeconomic developments drive democracy. As the economy and society become diverse and dynamic, an authoritarian government cannot effectively manage all the challenges. It must give way to an open system, governing with the consensus of the governed and with the institutionalized participation of the citizens. The social requisites for democracy, as argued by various studies, include a relatively high level of economic development, literacy and education, industrialization, and communication, among others (Lipset, 1959). The actor-centered approach is most notably represented by the "transition school," which looks at democratization as a matter of elite operations. If political elites commit to democracy, democratic institutions, such as competitive elections and constitutional government, can be built by conscious effort. In fact, it can happen in places with no socioeconomic requisites for democracy, such as in 1989 in Mongolia (Fish, 1998). As Huntington (1991) argues, democracies are created not by causes, but by the "causer."

What the transition arguments fail to point out is that political choices of the elite are structured by the situations in which they find themselves. These situations, above all, depend on socioeconomic development. In this regard, the modernization theories of democratization—arguing for preconditions of democracy—certainly have a point. But people who argue for the social prerequisites of democracy, the classical modernization theorists, miss one important point. Socioeconomic variables, however important, do not explain how certain structural factors translate into political outcomes. For example, it is frequently argued that one favorable condition for democracy is a relatively high proportion of educated middle class. But one must go beyond this and ask why when the society has a strong middle class, political elites would make choices that lead to democratic reforms. Notably, an educated middle class favors democracy because such democratic institutions favor the market in the economic arena. Such preferences of a big portion of the population present the elite with pressure to reform institutions. In the end, structural factors do not produce democratic reforms; it is the political demands resulting from a certain social structure that matter.

In fact, the link between these two major schools of thought lies in public attitudes about democracy. Elites make decisions by assessing how the public will react to various political agendas. How the public will receive a certain political agenda depends on the values of the public. Above all, their attitudes and values determine public political preferences. The connection between social structural factors and elite behaviors is, in the end, the people. This is to say, it is true that economic development and modernization promote democracy, but they promote democracy by producing a public that demands democratic institutions. Value change comes along with expanding markets and social mobilization. Economic development, industrialization, marketization, and expansion of social interaction by individuals all work to promote prodemocratic attitudes of the public. Such attitudes then translate into pressures on the political elite to introduce democratic reform and liberalization. In this sense, a third school of comparative democratization study, the study of prodemocratic values, offers the link between a structural perspective and the elite-pacting perspective.

A Conceptual Framework

In light of these considerations, I propose a conceptual framework to understand democratic transition and consolidation. Our study of democratization suffers from a profusion of academic works on the subject. A conceptual framework will provide a coherent perspective, and I propose a conceptual framework that links the three major schools of democratic studies: the modernization school, the elite-pacting school, and the democratic values school. Of these three schools, I argue the examination of citizen values provides the most direct evidence of democratic transition. The people will come to demand democracy, and in so doing, they will win democracy. Socioeconomic modernization affects human attitudes and behaviors, which in turn change politics, and elites will conduct state affairs according to the kinds of pressures they perceive from the citizenry. This framework, which has several important components, appears in the following figure.

Modernization: Economic Development and Social Changes

Modernization theory is relevant in that economic growth drives social change and institutional adaptations. In my framework, socioeconomic modernization includes economic growth and social changes. Social changes may include the emergence and growth of a middle class, urbanization, expanded literacy and education levels, emergence and growth of a capitalist class, and others. Changes also occur in formal institutions in a society; for example, institutionalization of the market process, emergence and proliferation of public media and emergence of a strong civil society in the form of nongovernmental organizations (NGOs).

Value Changes—It's the People!

Socioeconomic developments must translate into changes in people's values and behaviors to have an effect on politics. Along with modernization come people's prodemocratic attitudes and values. Significantly, we should differentiate among three kinds of attitudes and values generally referred to as prodemocratic: self-expression values, support for democracy, and civic culture. Each has a different conceptual emphasis and should be treated differently to truly understand the relationship between value

Figure 2.1. A framework for the study of democratization.

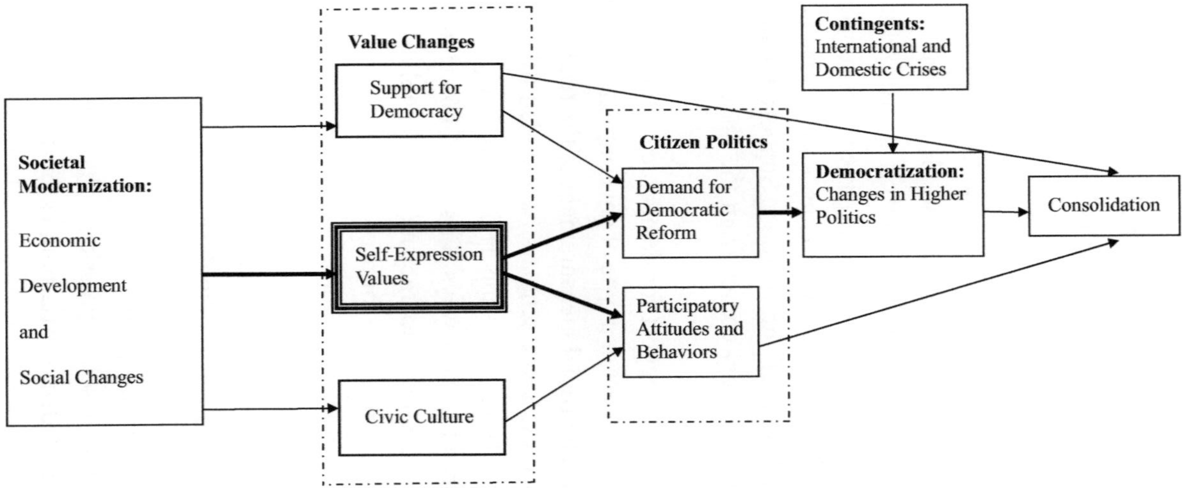

changes and the emergence, consolidation, and performance of democracy. I will offer a thorough review of the relevant literature in chapter 2. A brief explanation of these concepts follows.

A. ***Support For Democracy***

Support for democracy in a modernizing society emerges after the public's exposure to the idea of democracy. Democracy first originated in the northwest corner of Europe, and has long thrived in the West. The emergence of support for democracy in a non-Western developing society results largely from global exchange of information. Support for democracy in a non-Western society comes from the dissemination of ideas of democracy.

People show support for democracy after they begin to consider it as a concept or a type of government, and this, in general, presents a superficial measurement of the readiness of a society for democracy. Some scholars have called this "lip service" to democracy. But strong support for democracy among the public are important in two ways. First, in a nondemocratic society, strong support for democracy means the public now consciously demands a democratic form of government. With such public demand, democratic reform will meet public support, while failure to reform may generate public discontent. Second, critical for the consolidation of a fledging democratic system, in a new democracy the system must enjoy high public support.

B. ***Self-Expression Values***

The concept of self-expression values offers a more concrete perception of democratic politics by the public. For example, an individual may be unaware of the idea of democracy, or her government may have convinced her that her country's system is superior to democracy. Under such circumstances one can still find out whether this individual has a strong aspiration for democracy. For example, if she considers protecting freedom of speech more important than maintaining state security, then her aspiration to democracy is real. In this sense, we can understand a readiness for democracy, as opposed to the support of democracy in many authoritarian societies, such as China, where the public often sees the word *democracy* portrayed as an American institution linked to imperialism by state propaganda. I will explain this point in more detail in the following chapter.

Furthermore, the concept of self-expression values is important not only because it normally translates into public demands for political reform toward more democratic government. It also indicates a public's active participation in civil society. In this way, it plays an important role in building social infrastructure for democracy.

This book focuses especially on self-expression values. In Figure 2.1, I use stronger lines for the box representing self-expression values to emphasize such a point. In later chapters I will first examine (1) how socioeconomic developments affect the rise of self-expression values (chapters 4 and 5). Then, my major effort will be to show how self-expression values affect citizen politics. I will show that (2) the presence of stronger self-expression values means citizens will more likely demand political changes: they are more critical of government and more likely to participate in elite-challenging politics (chapters 6 and 8). Furthermore, (3) the presence of stronger self-expression values also means citizens participate more actively in civil society (chapter 7). Stronger arrows mark these causal relations in Figure 2.1.

C. ***Civic Culture***

The classical notion of the term *prodemocratic values* refers to the set of values originally known as civic culture. Civic culture refers to trust, tolerance, and participatory attitudes. Earlier, civic culture meant a necessary condition for the quality of democracy (Almond & Verba, 1963). More recently the term has come to mean a factor that affects democratic consolidation. This is most notably presented by scholarship on performance or quality of democracy, such as the social capital theory of Putnam (1993, 2000) and the new civic culture theory of Inglehart (1990). In my framework, I argue civic attitudes contribute to citizen's participation in local and national governmental or nongovernmental activities. Once democratic transition has taken place, civic culture is important for democratic consolidation, but a high level of civic culture does not directly lead to demand for democracy.

Citizen Politics

How citizens engage in politics reflects their values and beliefs, although institutional factors will also matter. In this framework, I list two types of citizen politics important for democracy. Demand for political reform refers to overt criticism and challenges of government by citizens. This, as I will show later, largely include two dimensions. One, citizens' elite-challenging attitudes, refers to distrust of government in my study. The other, citizens' elite-challenging behaviors, refers to protest in my study. Other scholars have variously called these attitudes and behaviors civil discontent, civil disobedience, or the like. The central notion, however, remains the same. The other type of citizen politics, civic engagement or participation in civil society, is especially noted for its importance for the performance of democracy and, for new democracies, democratic consolidation (Diamond, 1997; Putnam, 1993). The rise of self-expression values affects both types of citizen politics. As my study will show, rising self-expression values mean people are more willing to criticize and challenge the government, and people also show more willingness to participate in civic groups and civil society.

Contingents

The term *contingents* refers to sudden events that have a substantial impact on the course of political development. In many countries, unexpected developments can expedite or delay the democratization process. For example, degradation of an economic situation or international crises can influence democratization significantly. Take, for example, the following illustration of how contingents can matter in political changes. The death of former Chinese Communist Party (CCP) Secretary Hu Yaobang became a contingent when it caused university students to take to the streets. The students' memorial of Hu quickly transformed into a large public demonstration demanding transparency in government. Eventually, the demonstration turned into a formal demand for democratization, including demands to replace the one-party regime with a multiparty democracy

(Zhao, 2000). Thus, the sudden death of an important political figure, something no one predicted, instigated a movement that put China at a crossroad between democracy and one-party rule.

Former President Chiang Ching-kuo of Taiwan in 1986 launched a series of political reforms that eventually democratized the authoritarian party-state. Observers believed his increasingly deteriorating health contributed to his decision to do so (Nathan & Ho, 1993), again illustrating the potentially critical factor of contingencies. Another example occurred in the early 1980s failure of the Argentine government in the war against Britain that led to governmental changes, among them the downfall of a military junta. Several scholars, when trying to conceptualize democratization, have pointed out the importance of such contingents. One scholar has conceptualized the process of democratization as "structured contingents" (Haynes, 2001), meaning, while structural factors are the more basic causes of political changes, contingents normally serve as the triggering factor.

Democratization: Changes in High Politics

Public demands for political liberalization can directly cause democratization. In a gradual manner, continued pressure on the government results in slow but constant relaxation of political control, such as the case of China. In more dramatic forms, an abrupt rise of large-scale popular discontent results in rapid transition from authoritarianism to democracy—as in the case of South Korea in 1987 and several major transitions in Eastern Europe in 1989. Here, democratization implies the change of government institutions. The transition eventually must come around to the arena of high politics: the ruling elite, which includes, almost always, hard-liners and soft-liners as well as reformers, and the opposition. In fact, the extensive body of scholarship called *transitology* predominantly concerns this part of the story of democratization (Friedman, 1994; Huntington, 1991; Linz & Stepan, 1996; O'Donnell, Schmitter, & Whitehead, 1986).

Democratic Consolidation

Democratization and consolidation comprise the output end of this conceptual framework. Since the late 1989 post-Communism transition, much research has focused on this issue. More and more scholars accept that transition from authoritarian rule does *not* necessarily lead to the consolidation of democracy (Carothers, 2002; O'Donnell, Schmitter, & Whitehead, 1986). In many cases the collapse of the old authoritarian regime has not meant the establishment of a democracy, but instead a sort of semiauthoritarianism (Ottaway, 2002). The consolidation of new democracies has become a subject of study itself, acquiring the title *consolidology.* By now a consensus seems to have emerged regarding the indispensable role of civil society: a strong civil society with dense and active networks can contribute significantly to democratic consolidation. In this sense, a participatory, trusting civic culture can contribute to democratic consolidation and the sustainability and quality of democracy. Such civil society groups, networks, and attitudes (such as trust and tolerance) come under the umbrella known as social capital, and this theoretic persuasion has resulted in projects of civil society and social capital development flourishing in the developing world.

Each of these constructs makes up an integral part in the study of democratization. But value changes become critically important in the dynamics leading to democratization. Past scholarship tended to emphasize either social prerequisites or actions of political players. Neither argument is wrong, but citizen politics, which depend on people's values, provide the key linkage between social prerequisites and elite behaviors. This argument will be discussed in later chapters, as concrete causal relationships are identified.

Chapter 3

Values and Democracy

While comparative studies of the relationship between citizen values and democracy have increased (see, e.g., Inglehart, 1997; Inglehart & Welzel, 2005; Dalton & Shin, 2007), we should separate the various kinds of values that matter to democracy. Very often, researchers use the term *prodemocratic value* with little differentiation. In fact we can identify at least three kinds of values normally called prodemocratic values. The first, *civic value,* refers to the values and attitudes important for the stability and performance of democratic institutions (Almond & Verba, 1963). The second, *support for democracy*, means preference for the democratic political system over other forms of government (Inglehart, 2003a). The third, a fairly new construct, generally reflects an individual's support for civic rights and liberty and a preference for expression over some traditional values such as material security and order. It has in various cases been called *self-expression values* (Inglehart & Baker, 2000; Welzel, Inglehart, & Klingemann, 2003), *liberty aspiration* (Welzel & Inglehart, 2005), and *libertarian values* (Flanagan & Lee, 2000), among others. In this book, this set of values is referred to as self-expression values.

To understand the rising demand for political democratization, we should pay the most attention to the third group, the self-expression values. This does not mean to downplay the importance of civic values and support for democracy, but those values, however, play a stronger role in democratic consolidation after the transition period. They do not necessarily lend themselves to examining the demand of political changes in a society still under authoritarian rule. Later in this chapter, I outline several research questions one might ask in understanding the rise of self-expression values in East Asia, and how changing values can help us understand the prospect of political changes.

CIVIC CULTURE AND SOCIAL CAPITAL

With due respect to de Tocqueville, the concept of civic culture has a more recent history starting in the 1960s (Almond & Verba, 1963), and finds its most recent incarnation in the works of Putnam (1993, 1995, 2000), Inglehart (1990, 1997), and Gibson (1992, 1996), among others. According to this stream of literature, interpersonal trust, tolerance of groups that one dislikes, and civic engagement (notably political participation and political efficacy) comprise the most important attitudes that make a democracy work. After breaking a new path for the study of political development, this line of inquiry in fact sees a diminishing explanatory power in light of recent findings in comparative democratization. Civic attitudes count, but generally they matter because they help consolidate newly democratized regimes (Brzezinski, 2001). One could hardly make the case that a society under authoritarian rule will likely democratize because its public has demonstrated strong civic attitudes (Inglehart, 1997).

Civic culture refers to a political culture in which citizens (1) trust their fellow citizens, (2) cooperate and reciprocate, (3) show tolerance of out-groups, (4) display competence in political participation, and (5) participate in civil and community activities (Inglehart, 1990; Putnam, 1993). Each of these qualities, however, is not a simple concept. For example, Almond and Verba (1963) mainly link political culture and democracy performance through citizens' civic competence, which means the ability of individual citizens to influence politics—either measured by behaviors or by self-perceptions. Almond and Verba (1963) also argue the importance of trusting and cooperative social relationships for civic competence and, in turn, for democracy performance: individuals have to cooperate to achieve political goals in a democracy. *Civic cooperation* refers to cooperative political behaviors, which are more likely to emerge in societies with higher interpersonal trust and responsiveness, more social interactions outside family and work group (sociability and networking), and more freedom of communication. In this light, organizational membership contributes to civic competence as it increases sociability and social networks. This point about organizational membership came originally from de Tocqueville and attracts heavy attention from scholars who use the terms *civil society* or *social capital* (Putnam, 1993; 2000).

For Inglehart (1977, 1990, 1997), civic culture is part of the syndrome called *postmaterialism* that contributes to the stability of democracy in advanced industrial societies. The rise of postmaterialism results from affluence generated by a sustained period of socioeconomic modernization. Generations who grow up (and socialize) in materially secure environments assume a value system that is different from those who suffer scarcity, uncertainty, and life threats. In general, a cultural shift takes place from materialism to postmaterialism. While *materialist* values stress maintaining economic growth, a strong defense, strong political leadership, a stable economy, and social order, postmaterialism stresses trust, tolerance, quality of life, participation in government, and free expression (Inglehart, 1990). Trust, overall life satisfaction, and negative support of revolution make up a civic culture highly supportive of democratic stability (Inglehart, 1988). Statistical analyses find postmaterialism highly correlates to democratic stability (Inglehart, 1997). The concept of *postmaterialism* has proven useful in understanding value changes as societies move from agrarian to industrial to postindustrial. It has, to a considerable degree, shaped the study of politics in advanced democracies (Gibbins, 1989).

Putnam's social capital theory (1993) marked another influential development in the civic culture tradition. Putnam first looked at the disparity in institutional performance he found among regional governments in Italy. In areas with a high level of civic involvement, the performance of the government tends to be better. In his definition, civic involvement does not mean direct participation in political actions (such as voting), but rather participation in civic organizations such as amateur sport clubs or choral societies. He defines civic culture as trust, tolerance, networks, and norms that enable citizens to act together more effectively to pursue shared goals. While such social capital represents the key to democratic stability and good performance of democratic governments, declining social capital results in the "disaffected" democracy of the U.S. (Pharr & Putnam, 2000). In India, social capital can help reduce ethnic conflicts (Varshney, 2002), and around the world, social capital, such as trust, is critical for social and economic development (Fukuyama, 1995). In fact, studies of civic culture and social capital (notably, trust and tolerance) and their importance to democracy have flourished from the 1990s into the early 2000s (Gibson, 2001; Lovell, 2001; Mishler & Rose, 1997; Misztal, 1996; Newton, 2001; Rose, 1994).

Yet, as much as civic culture or social capital matters to democracy, it does so by increasing social cohesiveness, reducing societal complexity, lubricating social cooperation, and increasing institutional legitimacy (Misztal, 1996). Hence, its impact on society and politics likely has the same effect regardless of regime type. While a high level of trust, tolerance, and civic engagement can help democratic consolidation and performance, it can probably also help an authoritarian regime consolidate and gain legitimacy. For example, although some people argue that civic values, such as trust, cannot flourish in authoritarian societies, studies have found that in places such as China and Vietnam, the level of interpersonal trust is actually very high (Dalton, Pham, Pham, & Ong, 2003). Thus, to call civic culture prodemocratic may in fact mislead. Instead, one may more accurately call these democracy-friendly or regime-friendly values. Democratic consolidation may well require a high level of civic culture and social capital, but civic culture cannot directly lead to democratization or instigate a breakaway from authoritarian rule.

SUPPORT FOR DEMOCRACY

A second group of values and attitudes frequently examined in the study of democracy, public support for democracy, represents the overt support of democracy over other forms of government. In measuring support for democracy, researchers tend to ask questions like "Do you agree or not that democracy is the best (or least bad) political system we can have?" or "Do you agree or not that an authoritarian political system may be better than a democratic system?" By so doing, public opinion surveys can gauge the level of mass support for democracy. For example, WVS found that in Albania and Egypt, 99% of those surveyed considered a democratic system a "very good" or "fairly good" way of governing their countries, while in Russia, only 62% said so (Inglehart, 2003a).

Support for democracy can measure different dimensions of attitudes toward democracy. For example, it can measure directly the desirability of a democratic system in an individual's mind. This we can call *regime preference*: whether an individual considers democracy a good form of government or whether she feels some other forms of government might be better. A person's understanding of the strengths and weaknesses of democracy add a related dimension. For example, some people may see democracy as an indecisive political system; others may feel that democracy may hinder economic development. All such attitudes may have important implications for politics, and many surveys have looked at measuring these public opinions.

For example, researchers found that in the Islamic world, a majority of the population express a preference of democracy over other forms of government, and a person's religion makes no difference in this regard (Norris & Inglehart, 2003; Tessler, 2003). Researchers have carried out similar research in Muslim countries in Central Asia (Rose, 2002). Klingemann (1999) created a democratic support index by combining a respondent's support for democracy attitudes and support for nondemocratic forms of government, which has been widely used in measuring support for democracy in various attitudinal studies.

This dimension of public support for democracy indicates how successfully the democratic system has taken hold. For new democracies, this becomes extremely important, as it means the "democratization of mass political orientations" (Shin & Park, 2003). A concern has arisen in new democracies regarding public support for democracy. For example, in many newly democratized countries and especially among the post-Soviet republics, a growing dissatisfaction toward democracy—a phenomenon called the *posthoneymoon effect* (Catterberg, 2002)—has cropped up. Similarly, in Korea and Taiwan—two East Asian democracies that emerged in the late 1980s—in the late 1990s the public developed an increasing dissatisfaction with democracy. So much so that, from 1996 to 1999, a slightly larger portion of people in Korea believed that "Sometimes authoritarianism is preferable to democracy," and the percentage agreeing "democracy is always preferable" decreased (Chu, Diamond, & Shin, 2001). In post-Communist Eastern Europe, satisfaction with new democracy largely occurs with better economic well-being brought by political change and a lingering fear of previous Communist regimes (Mishler & Rose, 1996).

Why Support for Democracy Is Not Enough

Public support for democracy is important in two ways. For one, a true democracy must enjoy high public support and participation. It cannot remain a polity with an alienated and politically indifferent public or flourish as a "disaffected democracy" (Pharr & Putnam, 2000). Significantly, new democracies must sustain a high level of public support for democracy (Chu, Diamond, & Shin, 2001), otherwise the consolidation process will falter. Secondly, in a society where democracy has yet to emerge, without a public generally supportive of the notion of democracy, democratization efforts will very likely be seen as irrelevant. But this construct may only have face validity if we want to know the real demand for democratic institutions. We need to take into account several problems. First, the overt measurement of individual opinions toward democracy largely depends on the individual's understanding of the term *democracy*. When we ask an individual whether he supports democracy, we assume that the individual understands the term. But situations occur when people do not actually have an understanding of the term *democracy* or what it really means to live in a democracy.

In a survey conducted in China in 1993, a question related to democratic reform asked: do you agree or disagree that, if we are to expand democracy in our country at the present moment, it will cause social instability? About 30% of those surveyed either did not understand the question or did not know how to answer. Furthermore, one third of rural respondents, and 44% of those with less than primary education, do not understand or do not know how to answer the question (Shi Tianjian, *Social Change and Social Value Survey*, 1993).

Asking people how they feel about democracy raises another problem. We assume that the word *democracy* holds a commonly accepted meaning across societies, but this assumption does not hold up. The ideas and practices of *dmokaraasi* in Senegal differ from those of America, England, and Canada (Schaffer, 1998) as they differ from the ideas the Chinese term for democracy, *minzhu,* carries. Literarily, *min* means people, *zhu* means master. In China, people see *minzhu* more as an ideal type of political system, not necessarily as the multiparty electoral politics practiced in the West (Nathan, 1985). In fact, some argue that *minzhu* in China equates to *the* ideal political system to which the Chinese people are entitled. As one scholar puts it, democracy "is expanded into a laundry list that contains almost all kinds of good things" (Hu, 2000, p. 4). Hence, the one-party regime in China continues to call itself a democratic government. Unsurprisingly, the Chinese public considers democracy a good thing: in a survey, 90% of the Chinese public agree or strongly agree that democracy represents the best form of political system (WVS, 2001).

Thus, overt support for democracy does not sufficiently gauge a society's demand for democracy. Furthermore, in an authoritarian society such as China, it is not possible to ask for people's overt support for democracy in the real sense of the term (such as asking whether people want multiparty elections in China). We need to explore indirect measurements of prodemocratic attitudes.

THE RISE OF SELF-EXPRESSION VALUES

Self-expression values offer the most promising concept for understanding the linkage between values and political change. We can trace the origin of this concept to postmaterialism, first advanced by Inglehart (1971). At that time, the materially secure social environment in post-World War II Europe had given rise to a drastic shift in mass values. Compared to the value orientation of earlier generations, Europeans who grew up amid the fast postwar economic growth tended to emphasize liberty, aesthetics, and expression values over economic development and social order, as well as a growth of interpersonal trust and tolerance. The rise of such values helps explain the stability of democracy in industrial societies (Inglehart, 1990). In these works Inglehart presented a revised definition of civic culture: for him, interpersonal trust, tolerance, and life satisfaction (or a sense of well-being) made up a civic culture that contributed to the stability and performance of democracy.

Into the 1990s, analysis of survey data from more than 40 societies around the world found more evidence that, as the economy develops, value change follows. Regardless of cultural specificities, value changes in different societies take a predictable pattern. In one dimension, people's values change from a survival orientation to a well-being orientation. While in a traditional society, where economic scarcity always looms, social norms emphasize conformity, respect for authority and order, and economic accumulation. As a society modernizes, the citizenry begins more and more to take its security for granted, and as a result strict social norms begin to dissolve. In a materially secure environment, maximizing economic gains and struggle for survival gradually fade from people's top priorities. Instead, people tend to favor overall well-being, such as quality of work experience and leisure. More importantly, as survival no longer presents a problem, people's aspirations shift toward expression, entitlement, and participation. Meanwhile, as social life becomes more diverse and dynamic, people become more tolerant (Inglehart, 1997). Such values are conducive to the development of democracy.

Self-Expression Values and Democracy

The value change from a *survival* to a *well-being* orientation is most aptly described as the outcome of modernization and postmodernization. The implication for politics is that, overall, the rise of new social values means the emergence of new political issues and new patterns of citizen politics. In his 1997 book, Inglehart left undeveloped the explanation of what such changes mean to democracy (see *Modernization and Postmodernization* [Inglehart, 1997].) At the time, the materialist/postmaterialist paradigm still dominated the discussion of political implications of value changes, as it had in the past (Abramson & Inglehart, 1995; Inglehart, 1977; Inglehart & Abramson, 1994). To the extent democracy was concerned, these discussions emphasized the role of postmodern values in stabilizing democracy. Scholars argued again and again that trust, tolerance, and a sense of overall life satisfaction together make a culture supportive of democracy (Inglehart, 1997), but the question of whether such value changes mean a higher possibility of democratic transition remained unexamined. In this sense, it served as a rediscovery for the civic culture tradition, where the stability and quality of democracy held court, not the likelihood of emerging democracy.

A more developed theory emerges with the advancement of the self-expression concept, which crystallizes a concept loosely referred to earlier as *well-being* values into five tightly correlated values: a postmaterialist orientation, tolerance, trust, political activism, and a sense of happiness (Inglehart & Baker, 2000). Cultures ranking high in one of these values tend to rank high in all the others. In general, traditional and agrarian societies normally score low in these values, while more modernized and postindustrial societies score much higher. Furthermore, a new linkage between value and democracy emerges. Self-expression values include tolerance, trust, political activism, and greater emphasis on freedom of speech as compared to economic security and social order. With the emphasis on freedom of speech, individual liberty, and political activism, the rise of self-expression values leads to "growing mass demands for liberalization in authoritarian societies, and to rising levels of direct mass participation in societies that are already democratic" (Inglehart, 2003a, p. 51). In an authoritarian society, mass demands for liberalization create pressure on the elites to introduce political change (Flanagan & Lee, 2000). Rising levels of direct mass participation in democratic societies thus give a higher quality to democracy, as argued repeatedly by writers in the social capital tradition (Putnam, 2000). In these two senses, research in prodemocratic values for the first time identify a set of values that can explain both the quality of democracy in a society already democratic and the strength of popular demand for democratization in an authoritarian society.

Empirical evidence supports this linkage. A self-expression variable calculated using the largest cross-cultural value survey data closely correlates with various indicators of democratic governance. The correlation between a society's level of self-expression values around 1995 and the accumulative score of that society's Freedom House score between 1990–2000 is a striking 0.83 or higher (Inglehart, 2003a).

Human Development, Freedom, and Political Institutions

At the aggregated level then, self-expression values correlate highly with the level of democracy of a given society. But how does this work out at the microlevel? Why do changes in individual values and worldviews mean a higher quality of democracy for a society? The answer comes with the human development theory of democratization, which Welzel first helped infuse into Inglehart's studies of value changes and democracy. Human development as normally known in development economics refers to societal changes that help develop human capacity: the empowerment of human beings to make wider choices in human life. In effect, human development equals the expansion of human freedom (Sen, 1999). The human development theory of democratization builds on Sen's idea of expansion of human freedom and conceptualizes human development as a comprehensive process much richer than the accumulation of economic security, wealth, and individual empowerments. This theory sees human development as comprising of three dimensions: socioeconomic development, value change, and democracy. Most scholars have limited their inquiries of human development to socioeconomic development—the first dimension, also frequently referred to as modernization (industrialization, urbanization, occupational differentiation, social mobilization, mass education, information revolution, and so on). Earlier literature treated the second dimension, value change, as the shift or the "silent revolution" from a traditional to a modern and postmodern culture. The rise of the self-expression values concept is the key element of this complex process of value change. A society's advancement in social and economic development will lead to value changes among the public toward more proliberty, profreedom, and protolerance. Amid changing social realities in terms of material conditions of human life and social values of the population, human development also means social and political institutions must adapt to such changes—hence the third component, the evolution and development of political institutions. This can be broadly understood as the rise of democracy as a universally accepted system of government: the evolution, development, or building of institutions for the protection and support of citizen's choices. Indeed, democratic legal and political institutions have two major functions contributing to human development as freedom. The first, to protect individual liberty, signifies the choice one makes for one's private life. The second provides infrastructure and assistance for participation in citizens' public choice making. The second function has equal importance, if not more, than the first because any public choices, in the forms of public policies, will affect each individual directly or indirectly (Inglehart & Welzel, 2005).

Two Linkages

The key to understanding this process of human development, which has as its political outcome the establishment of democratic institution, lies in two causal linkages that connect the material, social, and political dimensions of human development: the *means–motives linkage* and the *motives–rules linkage* (Welzel, Inglehart, & Klingemann, 2003). Means–motives linkage explains how economic development gives rise to self-expression values. Economic security and affluence are the preconditions of the emergence of proliberty, prorights values. Before modernization, lack of resources restricts human autonomy, and people must consciously or unconsciously adapt their aspiration to such restrictions. But economic development makes it possible for individuals to pursue self-expression and self-realization. Earlier studies (Inglehart, 1977, 1988, 1990, 1997) have identified this mechanism: economic development and affluence in material resources give rise to a set of values that stresses tolerance, freedom of speech, and participatory opportunities and rights. These values manifest people's motivation for political involvement. "In all nations, citizens appear to convert socioeconomic resources into political involvement" (Verba, Nie, & Kim, 1978, p. 73). Socioeconomic resources determine a person's capacity for political involvement. Empirical evidence shows that socioeconomic development generates a high level of individual liberty aspirations, a measurement of the priority a person assigns to the protection of free speech and to the opportunities to participate in politics (Inglehart & Welzel, 2005).

Such motivations and aspirations turn into public preferences and demands for democratic institutions at the societal level: the motives–rules linkage that connects values with institutional changes. In an authoritarian society, the regime may enjoy considerable legitimacy when mass preference leans toward security, order, and economic growth. But with the public increasingly emphasizing self-expression and individual freedom over other values, they more and more see as illegitimate the institutions that restrict their rights. In this way, the growing self-expression values (the motives) become the demand for political changes toward more open and democratic rules (the rules) in an authoritarian society (Welzel, Inglehart, & Klingemann, 2003). This mechanism works similarly in a democratic society, in that increased emphasis of self-expression turns into public demand for a higher quality of democratic institutions, and people's rights will be more effectively protected and provided.

This represents a significant advancement to earlier modernization theories. It goes beyond social changes at the aggregated level and offers linkages at the individual level. Thus, it integrates some major human projects—universal human rights, human development, and democracy, for example—into a single framework. Apparently, the emergence of the self-expression values concept makes up the centerpiece in this theory of democratization and human development. Globally, the level of individual resources explains 81% of the strength of self-expression values of a certain society, and the strength of self-expression values explains 75% of the degree of effective democracy of a certain society (Welzel, Inglehart, & Klingemann, 2003).

Self-Expression Values and Democratization in East Asia

No one will debate the fact that East Asia has pulled off one of the most successful stories of economic development in the world's history. We can debate with intense contention, however, whether and how economic development has brought political changes. For example, some argue that economic development in Asia, impressive as it is, will not bring democratic government (think Singapore). Others argue that good economic performance such as China's can actually enhance the legitimacy of the government in power. Hence, the success either allows the regime to ignore demands for political openness or simply discounts democracy as an alternative for the public to consider (de Mesquita & Downs, 2005). By examining the development of self-expression values and democracy, in the following chapters of this book I seek to contribute to the progress of this scholarly enterprise.

This task will unfold in two steps. First, I will demonstrate the linkage between East Asia's extraordinary economic growth record and the rise of self-expression values in this region. After showing that East Asian publics have become more and more self-expression-oriented, the second step will show that such value changes have significant implications for the rise of democracy. In fact, the analysis will show that the increasing proliberty, prorights publics in these societies have contributed greatly to the democratization of some societies in this region, and have fundamentally changed the political landscapes of societies yet to democratize, such as China and Vietnam.

Chapters 4 and 5 will show that in the last decades, economic developments have led to the rise of self-expression values among East Asia's publics. But how do value changes translate into changes in politics? How do we measure the pressure on elites for political change? We can measure individual willingness to participate in protest actions, such as signing a petition, joining a boycott, and joining a demonstration (Flanagan & Lee, 2000). If we can find a positive relation between a higher level of self-expression values and a higher potential for protest, then increased self-expression values mean increased likelihood of pressure on the government. A second variable, and probably a more direct one, is an individual's distrust of government. One could argue that in a place like China, with an overly authoritarian and coercive government, distrust of government equals a willingness to support or demand political change.

An examination of social capital can tell us how value change can contribute to the quality of democracy. We can measure social capital by observing people's participation in civic, social, and professional organizations. The existence and the viability of a civil society made up of nongovernmental organizations (NGOs) provide a linkage between individual citizens and the state. This is one important condition that makes a democracy work. On the other hand, participation in NGOs enables individual citizens to develop social and political skills for self-government and political participation. In other words, it increases citizens' civic competence and political efficacy. In this way, social capital helps improve the quality of democracy from below. The second major research question of this study asks whether self-expression values affect people's likelihood to participate in NGOs. Chapters 6, 7, and 8 will present these empirical examinations: the effect of self-expression values on people's protest behaviors, participation in civic organizations, and political trust, respectively. After these analyses at the microlevel, chapter 9 presents an aggregated-level analysis, predicting how fast the rise of self-expression values will lead to political liberalization in China. A truly democratic East Asia is actually not far away.

Part II

The Rise of Self-Expression Values

Chapter 4

Value Changes in Modernizing East Asia: The Self-Expression Phenomenon

The rise of a more secular, proexpression, and proliberty public in various countries has contributed to the global rise of democracy, especially since the late 1970s. As mentioned earlier, we know these social values as self-expression values (Inglehart & Welzel, 2005). To examine whether self-expression values are on the rise in East Asia and how such values change the political landscape there, we must first find out how we can best measure this value change. In the study of political culture and democratic attitudes, many scholars have proposed various ways to accomplish this. In this chapter, I first show how we can measure self-expression values among the six East Asian countries studied in this book. We can then use this measurement to examine the changes in this value dimension among the citizens in these societies in the last decades.

MEASURING SELF-EXPRESSION VALUES IN EAST ASIA

The literature to date defines self-expression values as a cluster of values that emerges as a society's degree of modernization/postmodernization increases. To capture this value change, scholars can design survey questions that gauge individuals' values and attitudes and then combine these survey variables into factor scores. The World Values Survey (WVS) was designed to gauge a comprehensive range of values and attitudes of people's across regions, cultures, ethnicities, religions, and other socio-economic categories (e.g., gender, age, and level of education). The WVS data set has, hence, provided scholars with a good repertoire of such value and attitudinal variables from which to find the best indicators of certain value phenomenon.

Inglehart & Welzel's construct of self-expression values—as developed through the years in various works (Inglehart, 1990; Inglehart & Baker, 2000; Inglehart, Welzel, & Klingamann, 2003; Inglehart & Welzel, 2005)—generally include five dimensions: liberty aspiration, life satisfaction, public expression, tolerance, and trust. Liberty aspiration refers to an individual's emphasis on liberty, free expression, and rights over material and physical security (e.g., economic security and personal safety). This has evolved from an earlier concept known as postmaterialism, and Welzel has recently stressed the importance of this dimension in understanding the public's demand for democratic openings in any society (Welzel, 2006). Life satisfaction refers to a person's overall sense of quality of life, normally represented in a person's sense of happiness or emphasis on leisure versus work as the main component of life. Public expression refers to a person's willingness to express his (mostly political) views with public behaviors, such as petitions, demonstrations, boycotts, sit-ins, and so on. Tolerance refers to a person's attitude toward socially disliked groups, whether the general public in the society tends toward inclusion or exclusion (Gibson, 1992). Homosexuals, prostitutes, minorities, immigrants, and people with generally unaccepted behaviors (e.g., drug users, ex-criminals, and heavy drinkers), serve as good examples of such disliked social groups. By asking an individual's attitudes about such people, in empirical research we can generally find out the degree of tolerance within a society. Lastly, trust refers to a person's perception of social environment: whether she sees that environment as trustworthy/safe or not. Social science literature stresses the importance of social or interpersonal trust to the performance of democracy, referring to it as an integral part of social capital (Misztal, 1996; Putnam, 1993; Warren, 2004).

This construct was created inductively by factoring a pooled WVS data set that includes four waves of surveys between 1981 and 2001, covering more than 60 societies around the world (Inglehart & Baker, 2000; Inglehart & Welzel, 2005). But at the same time, separately, other literatures support these value dimensions as consequential for the establishment and functioning of democracy (such as the literature's stresses on tolerance and trust). In the years to come, the debates on how social values affect democracy will likely center on these value dimensions.

But nevertheless, at the time of this study's publication, all the analyses have been conducted at the societal level. That is, these analyses use nations as units of analysis and examine the correlation between values & democracy among about 60 nation-states around the world (Inglehart & Baker, 2000; Inglehart & Welzel, 2005). The current study mainly hopes to determine the relation between values and politics at the individual level. Accordingly, moving from such a global analysis to individual-level analysis within a specific cultural region (East Asia), the search for an effective measurement of self-expression values needs to be pursued further. Furthermore, East Asia offers unique cultural specificities, such as the argument that the Confucian heritage stresses family, group, and authority over individual freedoms, for example (Park & Shin, 2006). Hence, in examining self-expression values in East Asia we need to look more carefully at value dimensions relating to such aspects of human life, which have generally been left out in the current literature on self-expression values.

Self-Expression Values in East Asia

To find the combination of variables representing self-expression values in East Asia, I also took an inductive approach by including as many relevant variables as possible and by allowing the emerging patterns to lead us to the best configuration of variables. I identified a pool of more than 20 variables from the WVS. The value concepts covered by these variables include the following items: liberty aspiration (e.g., whether political rights and freedom are more important than material interests), attitudes toward workplace authority (e.g., whether one should follow order unconditionally), attitudes toward family authority relationship (e.g., authority relationship between parents and children), attitudes toward gender equality, interpersonal trust, tolerance of out-groups, environmentalist beliefs (e.g., whether it is acceptable to sacrifice environment for economic development), attitudes toward religion (e.g., whether God is very important), attitudes towards one's personal life (e.g., whether friends are very important and whether leisure is very important), and political engagement (e.g., whether politics is very important). I based the selection of this large pool of variables on three lines of existing literature: the Asian values debate (Chan, 1998; Song, 2002; Tu, 2000a), the modernization of human values and individual modernity literature (Inkeles, 1966), and the literature of modernization, postmodernization, and democratic attitudes (Gibbins, 1989; Gibson, 1996; Inglehart, 1997; Inglehart & Baker, 2000). According to the literature, modernization affects all of the selected value dimensions and reflects the degree of democratic orientation of an individual or a public.

I conducted intensive analyses to find out which variables cluster to form cohesive factors. I adopted several criteria when selecting the variables that potentially constitute our self-expression values factor. Most importantly, given that liberty aspiration (or postmaterialism) is the main component of self-expressive orientation (Inglehart & Welzel 2005), I made it the core variable in the factor structure. If a variable has a high covariance with liberty aspiration, then it likely will have a high loading when included in the factor analysis with liberty aspiration. This would increase its probability of becoming part of our self-expression values factor. Social tolerance is highly correlated with liberty aspiration; these two variables therefore became the core components of our self-expression values factor.

In addition to liberty aspiration and tolerance, this measurement includes four themes not found in the self-expression values in the literature. More related to an individual's attitudes about family relationship and authority, these can be viewed as East Asia-specific value dimensions: rejection of patriarchy, rejection of paternalism, support for gender equality, and importance of leisure. Rejection of patriarchy is measured by the inclination towards equality in the parent–child relationship. It is reflected in the responses to statements about whether children's respect for parents ought to be earned, rather than expected, and whether parents should have their own lives to live, rather than living their lives entirely for their children. Rejection of hierarchic authority at the workplace is gauged by the question of whether one should question the logic and reasonableness of instructions before following them, or that one should always follow instructions unconditionally. In short, these elements of self-expression values correspond to an emphasis on independence, autonomy, and rationality, as opposed to blind obedience and deference to authority.

Another dimension in this self-expression factor is gender equality, as measured by responses to statements such as whether "men make better political leaders," "a boy's education is more important than a girl's," as well as attitude towards women having a career and women having the right to make their own marital, sexual, maternal choices. A favorable attitude towards gender equality is part of the fundamental value change accompanying the modernization process, and the move towards protection of women's rights is a good indicator of a shift towards a more prodemocratic worldview (Inglehart & Norris, 2003). The last dimension relates to the importance of leisure, which measures the shift from an outlook focused on material security to one geared toward a postmaterialist concern such as quality of life (Inglehart, 1990).

I combined these items into a factor analysis to identify if a common dimension of values occurs (Table 4.1). My final self-expression values measure includes attitudes toward liberty, participation, tolerance, gender equality, family, and workplace authority and questions that might be significantly related to this underlying dimension. Within East Asian societies, one sees significant coherence among these social values, although this may not always appear obvious at first glance. For instance, a person who considers freedom of speech more important than economic well-being will, among other things, also think: that men and women should enjoy equal social opportunities; that disliked groups or behaviors should be tolerated; that the relation between parents and children should not be patriarchal; and that paternalism at the workplace should be replaced by persuasion, negotiation, and mutual respect.

I excluded public expression in my analysis as part of the self-expression values factor because I consider public expression (protest) more of an individual's behavior than her attitudes. In fact, in a later chapter I will examine the impact of self-expression values on an individual's protest potential. Nevertheless, the liberty aspiration dimension in the current factor does relate to attitudes pertaining to political participation. The last three dimensions of my self-expression factor include rejection of paternalism, rejection of patriarchy, and support for gender equality.

To better understand the concept of self-expression values, we may look at how it correlates with other value dimensions. In Table 4.2, the upper panel comprises those values positively

Table 4.1. Factor structure of self-expression values in Confucian Asia.

	Loading
Liberty aspiration	
Give more priority to liberty and freedom than material and physical security.	.524
Tolerance	
Feel that behaviors such as abortion and groups such as prostitutes and homosexuals are somewhat justified.	.666
Equal family relationship	
Think that parents should earn respect by their behavior, instead of requiring children to respect them unconditionally; Think parents have their own life, instead of doing everything for the benefit of their children.	.658
Leisure is important	
Feel leisure is an important part of one's life.	.464
Gender equality	
Disagree that men have more right to jobs than women.	.328
Reject workplace paternalism	
Think that one should follow directions from one's supervisor only when one is convinced, instead of following directions unconditionally.	.305

Source. Fourth Wave (1999–2001) of WVS conducted in China, Japan, Korea, Singapore, and Vietnam; and the Third Wave (1995) of the WVS conducted in Taiwan. Extraction method: principal component analysis; one component extracted.

correlated with the self-expression factor, while the lower panel lists those dimensions negatively correlated with it.

This table displays self-expression values as a syndrome of values that emphasizes independence, creativity, liberty, and self-realization, while rejecting obedience, patriarchy, and paternalism (positive correlation with the item 2 in the table, negative correlation with items 7 and 8). It also stresses tolerance (negative correlation with item 10), gender equality (items 3, 4, 5, and 6), and quality of life (positive correlation with item 1, negative correlation item 9). Furthermore, self-expression values support secular rather than religious values (negative correlation with items 12 and 13) (Inglehart & Norris, 2004). Just as interesting is the finding that self-expression values run counter to strong nationalist sentiments (negative correlation with the last two items).

Nationalism in East Asia, a Side Note to Democratization

While industrialization of the modern age in West Europe evolved with rising nationalism (Hobsbawm, 1962), the age of postindustrialization and postmodernization sees the rise of so-called postmodern values such as environmentalism, support of different lifestyles (e.g., gay marriage), and cosmopolitanism. With this comes a decline in nationalist sentiment (see Inglehart, 1997), vindicated by the high (negative) correlation between items 14 and 15 and self-expression values in Table 4.2. More self-expression-oriented people are less willing to fight for their country in a war, and they tend to feel a lesser sense of national pride (rejecting nationalism).

The reason that these two variables do not factor in the self-expression indicator, despite the high correlations, should be

Table 4.2. Correlation between self-expression values and other attitudes.

Variables	*Correlation with Self-Expression Values*
Positively Correlated	
1. R thinks friends are important for one's life	0.237
2. R thinks independence is an important quality for children	0.123
3. R disagrees that women need to have children in order to feel fulfilled	0.140
4. R agrees that both husband and wife should contribute to household income	0.162
5. R disagrees that men make better political leaders than women	0.225
6. R disagrees that a boy education is more important than a girl's	0.186
Negatively Correlated	
7. One of R's life goals is to make R's parents proud	–0.156
8. R thinks obedience is an important quality for children	–0.229
9. R thinks hard work is an important quality for children	–0.249
10. R does not want to have heavy drinkers as one's neighbors	–0.208
11. R thinks good and evil can be clearly cut	–0.154
12. R is religious	–0.129
13. R thinks God is very important	–0.144
14. R is willing to fight in war for R's country	–0.300
15. R is proud about one's nation	–0.250

Source. Fourth Wave (1999–2001) of WVS conducted in China, Japan, Korea, Singapore, and Vietnam; and the Third Wave (1995) of WVS conducted in Taiwan, with a sample size of 1,500 for each country.
*All correlations significant at 0.001 level.

found in the history of nationalism in the particular region. Both China and Vietnam have been under Communist rule for a long period until recently. As a result, citizens under both regimes have lived through intense political education that emphasizes nationalism (Doolin & Ridley, 1968; Gilliom, 1978; G. Liu, 1998). Also, both countries went through several major wars in their histories, including some very recent ones (the Sino-Vietnam war of the late 1970s through the mid-1980s, the U.S.–Vietnam War of the 1960s and 1970s). In fact, in our current examination, the publics in China and Vietnam score highest in their readiness to fight for their country in a war.[1] On the other hand, Singapore, Taiwan, and South Korea, have (until recently also) lived in very insecure international environments (although for different reasons). As a result, the regime in each of these countries has stressed national solidarity while cultivating a sense of responsibility for its subjects to fight in wars. Thus the nationalist mentality in these countries undergone state intervention. That is probably why its changing pattern does not mesh with that of self-expression values.[2]

On another account, however, this does point to the importance of security in democratization. The interaction between internal development and external influence affects democratization, in the way that the public may give more priority to physical security than to a democratic system. In this regard, the rise of self-expression values also requires a secure international environment. Within this region, Singapore has a difficult history of resisting Communism from the north and maintaining independent nationhood in a geopolitical environment full of perceived security threats. South Korea's precarious survival has always borne the yoke of North Korea. Similarly, Taiwan faced the possibility of war with the mainland until well into the 1980s.

As some have argued, the democratization of Taiwan and Korea actually came later than the level of their socioeconomic development would have made possible. Similarly, Singapore, despite a very high level of modernization, remains authoritarian. Facing a threatening international environment, people show more willingness to accept an oppressive regime in so far as the public perceives that the regime provides protection. Indeed, democratization took place in this region only after major security threats had receded in the late 1980s. This, from the contrary side, supports the argument that prodemocratic self-expression values depend on the existence of material and physical security.

Is There a Confucian Asia? Are There Asian Values?

Earlier works have used a cultural map to position different societies around the word into so-called cultural zones or civilizations. These exercises normally find that Confucian countries, despite substantial intraregional differences, tend to cluster on the map. The map, drawn in two dimensions, includes the self-expression/survival dimension and the traditional/rational dimension (Inglehart, 2003b; Inglehart & Baker, 2000).

Besides this descriptive way to show the cultural cohesiveness of individual civilizations, we can test the existence of a Confucian Asia in three ways. This is possible now that we have come to a factor structure for self-expression values from the Confucian Asia survey data. The first way compares each of the six variables included in the self-expression values factor between different cultural zones. We could compare Confucian Asia with other parts of Asia—South Asia and non-Confucian East and Southeast Asia—given the existence of data from those societies.

However, given that values change and that change takes place with economic and human development, it would be wrong simply to compare a society's' values and beliefs without taking into account socioeconomic variables. For example, one cannot surmise by the simple fact that on average, people in Japan are less paternalistic at workplace than people in Burma, and say that the two cultures belong to two different belief systems (civilizations). The difference lies probably less in the fact that the two societies hold different belief systems, but more in the fact that one country has gone through decades of fast economic growth, while the other has remained an agrarian society.

We can disentangle such arguments by using analyses where we control the socioeconomic variables; hence the second way to test the existence of different civilizations. Regression analyses can discover significant differences between so-called Confucian countries and other countries after we control socioeconomic factors, such as the following, among others:

- GDP per capita (economic well-being)
- Share of industrial output in national output (degree of industrialization)
- Share of service industry in GDP (degree of postindustrialization)
- Female literacy level (human development)
- Number of doctors per thousand citizens (human development)
- Number of telephone/TV sets per thousand people (information)

In short, after controlling degree of modernization and human development, we can probably detect any real differences in people's belief systems.

The easier and third way, however, detects whether similar cultural patterns exist in other civilizations by running a factor analysis of the same variables on other countries. If, say, variables A, B, C, D, and E turn out to form a coherent factor in a set of societies (S), we can say we observe a certain cultural pattern in S societies. Then, we conduct a factor analysis of the same variables (A through E) in another set of societies (S') to see whether similar factor patterns emerge. If the two analyses result in different factor patterns, we can say that the two sets of societies belong to different cultures and that they have somewhat different belief systems.

Here we see this exercise performed on Confucian Asia and several South and Southeast Asian countries for which survey data exist, and conduct factor analyses of the variables identified to represent self-expression values in Confucian countries (Table 4.1) in the Philippines, Indonesia, India, and Bangladesh.

At first glance, this table does show that the factor structures of those non-Confucian countries differ somewhat from those of Confucian Asia. Based on these differences, we could probably say that indeed, something called "Asian Values" exists. But are these differences important? Granted, this exercise set out to test the existence of something called "Asian Values," which some of the political leaders in these countries have used to justify their political systems. What remains important for a political scientist then, is to ask, if such values exist that support an authoritarian form of government, are these values changing? If, say, patriarchy and paternalism belong to the core of "Asian Values," how have they changed within the current rapid socioeconomic developments. In this regard, it does not matter whether there is

Table 4.3. Factor loadings for Asia's non-Confucian societies.*

	C.Cs.	*INDSS*	*PLPSS*	*IND*	*BGL*
Liberty aspiration					
Give more priority to liberty and freedom than material and physical security.	.524	.363	.400	.639	.624
Tolerance					
Feel that behaviors such as abortion and groups such as prostitutes and homosexuals are somewhat justified.	.666	–[a]	–[a]	–[a]	.624[b]
Equal family relationship					
Think that parents should earn respect by their behavior, instead of requiring children to respect them unconditionally;					
Think parents have their own life, instead of doing everything for the benefits of their children.	.658	–[a]	–.331	.545	.598
Leisure is important					
Feel leisure is an important part of one's life.	.464	–.419	.456	–[a]	–[a]

(continued)

Table 4.3. *(continued)* Factor loadings for Asia's non-Confucian societies.*

	C.Cs.	*INDSS*	*PLPSS*	*IND*	*BGL*
Gender equality					
Disagree that men have more right to jobs than women.	.328	.681	.482	.514	–[a]
Reject workplace paternalism					
Think that one should follow directions from one's supervisor only when one is convinced, instead of following directions unconditionally.	.305	.590	.656	.547	–[a]
Number of component(s) extracted	1	3	3	2	2

Source. For Confucian countries, Fourth Wave (1999–2001) of WVS conducted in China, Japan, Korea, Singapore, and Vietnam; and the Third Wave (1995) of WVS conducted in Taiwan; for each of the other countries, the Fourth Wave WVS conducted in 1999–2000; with a sample size of 1,500 for each country.

[a]Loading lower than 0.30.

[b]The factor of tolerance in Bangladesh has a different structure compared to the Confucian societies and India. For a discussion, see Inglehart & Pippa, 2003.

*Countries in this table: C.Cs.: Confucian Countries; INDS: Indonesia; PLPS: Philippines; IND: India; and BGLD: Bangladesh.

a Confucian Asia or not; it does matter whether there is a rise in attitudes such as proliberty, tolerance, antipatriarchy, anti-paternalism, progender equality, and so on.

Self-Expression Values and Democracy

In this section, I look at how self-expression values change in East Asia. The ideal approach to such a question would require we review several decades of survey data to display changes through time. Here, we can give a partial examination to long-term trends in two of these societies. For Korea and Japan, where the WVS has been conducted ever since the First Wave, we do have data covering between 1981 and 2000. As the WVS has evolved through the years, several variables now used to measure the self-expression phenomenon did not appear in earlier surveys. This makes a strict comparison of the through-time change of self-expression values in the six-variable form impossible. Nevertheless, a factor score including three variables measured in all these surveys can be calculated and compared (Figure 4.1).

Figure 4.1 displays a factor score that includes the three variables measured in the surveys of 1981, 1990, and 2000: liberty aspiration, tolerance, and patriarchal family relations. The trend travels visibly upward. Korean society saw an increase in self-expression values similar to that of Japan between 1981 and 1990. However, between 1990 and 2000, while we see a steep increase in Japan, the trend of Korea is flat. We can probably attribute this to the fact that only three variables are included. Indeed, we focus on an examination between the two surveys of 1990 and 2000. As five of the six variables are measured in

Figure 4.1. Self-expression values in Japan and Korea over 20 years.

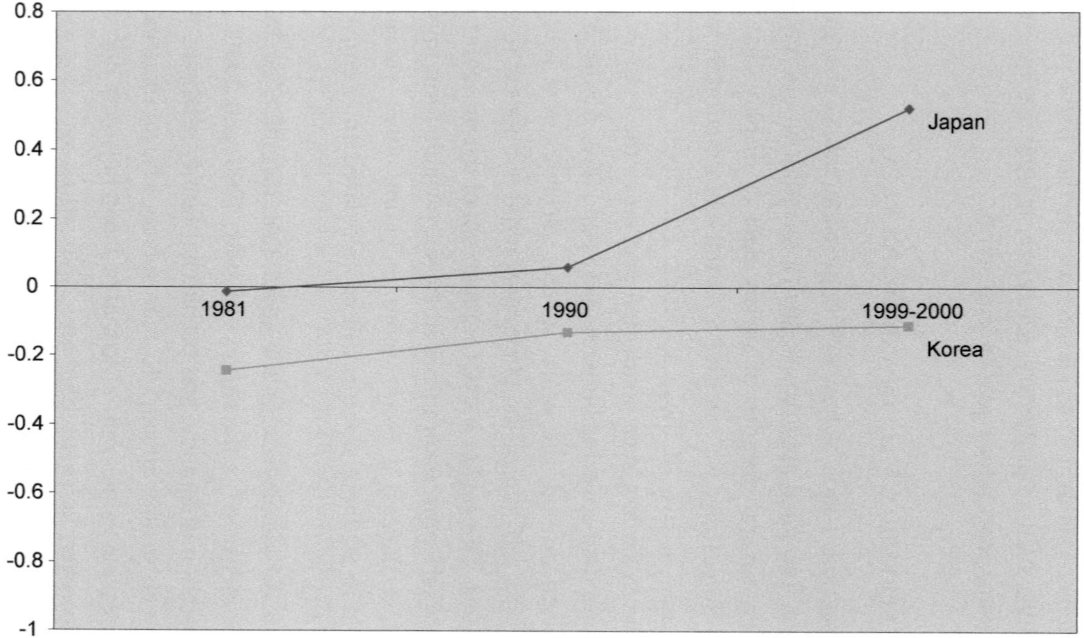

Source. 1981, 1990, 1999–2001 WVS of Japan and Korea.

Note. Factors for self-expression values include liberty aspiration, tolerance, and patriarchal family relations.

both surveys, we can generate and compare a more inclusive self-expression factor (Figure 4.2).

We see, then, an identifiable increasing trend in these two societies in the course of 20 years. The increase in Korea between 1990 and 2000 appears modest, especially in comparison with that of Japan; however, probably not because the increase in Korea is too small, but probably because the increase in Japan becomes exaggerated during the mathematical process that generated the factor scores.[3] Another reason may be that during 1990 to 2000, Koreans lived through a terrible economic downturn following the 1997 Asian financial crisis. This, no doubt, interrupted the increase in self-expression values observed during the 1981–1990 period.

At any rate, 10 years does not make up a sufficiently long period for big changes to occur in a society's belief systems. We can obtain a better sense of long-term trends and relationships between socioeconomic modernization and value changes in two systematic ways. The first looks at global value change patterns as affected by socioeconomic modernization. This allows us to use different countries as units of analysis and to determine the effect of socioeconomic indicators on value changes. The second looks at intergenerational changes among specific societies. For the six Confucian societies in our study, if we compare the generational differences of values and beliefs, we might grasp the trends of value changes in a period of the previous 50–60 years. We conduct these two analyses below.

Socioeconomic Modernization and Self-Expression Values

In this section I test the theory that socioeconomic modernization or the progress in overall human development causes

Figure 4.2. Self-expression values in Korea and Japan, 1990–2001.

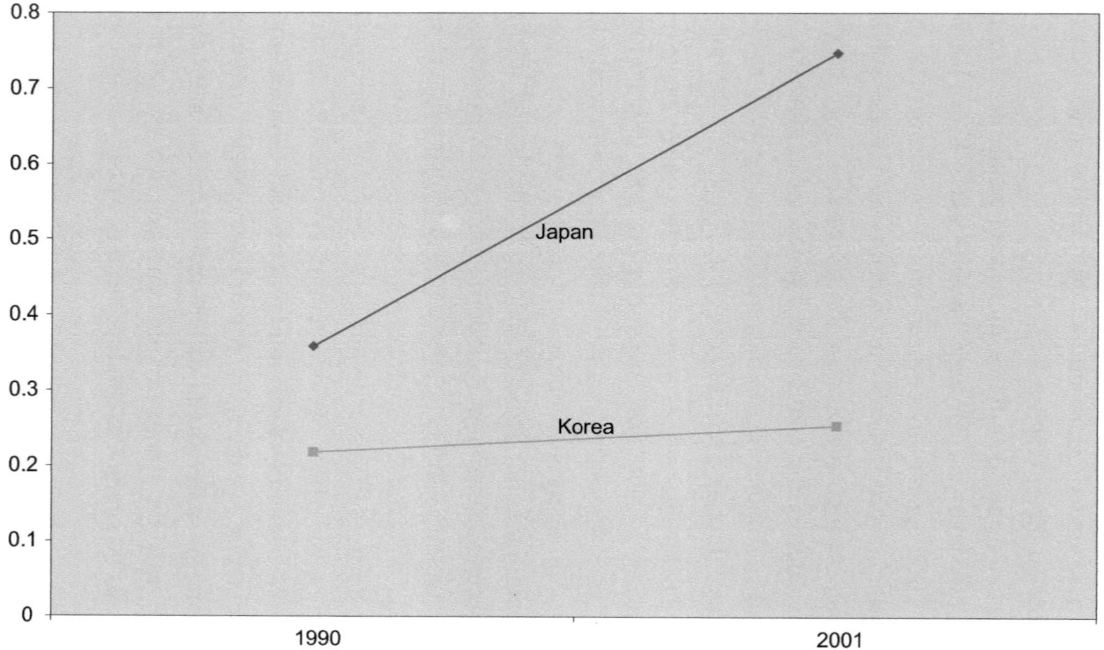

Source. 1990, 1999–2001 WVS of Japan and Korea.

Note. Factors for self-expression values include liberty aspiration, tolerance, progender equality, rejecting paternalism, and patriarchal family relations.

the rise of self-expression values. Here I move temporarily into analyses at the nation level, using societies as units of analysis. I first calculate a self-expression values score for all the countries for which we have survey data from either the 1999–2001 or 1995–1997 survey. This results in a database of about 80 cases. I then use several major socioeconomic indicators obtained from the World Development Indicators (WDI) of the World Bank (2002), and conduct the following analyses (Table 4.4).

These regression analyses show that economic development, postindustrialization, and overall level of human development (as measured by economic wealth and other social development indicators such as mass information) have positive effects on the level of self-expression values. This is, of course, not surprising, given earlier scholarship linking value changes to socioeconomic modernizations. Nonetheless, from this cross-national analysis we can draw some hypotheses for within-country examinations. Specifically, we should expect continued socioeconomic modernization would result in a more self-expression-oriented public. Such a hypothesis has very significant implications for our six East Asian societies, as several of them have enjoyed fast socioeconomic modernization. Furthermore, because value change takes place by generational replacement, we would expect that, in these fast-growing societies, younger generations would demonstrate stronger self-expression values than older generations. And, the generational gaps would be greater in countries where socioeconomic modernizations came faster, while countries with a slower rate of socioeconomic modernization would display very limited differences between younger and older generations. Let's put these hypotheses to the test.

Table 4.4. Socioeconomic modernization and self-expression.

	Dependent Variable: Strength of Self-Expression Values Around 2000[#]			
	Model 1	*Model 2*	*Model 3*	*Model 4*
GNI per capita 1995[a]	.093***	.094***	.078***	.055***
	(.009)	(.016)	(.011)	(.014)
Percentage of labor force	.129*	–.039		
in industry 1995[b]	(.067)	(.075)		
Percentage of labor force		.208**	.201**	.187**
in service sector 1995[c]		(.066)	(.064)	(.068)
Number of daily				.002*
newspapers per				(.001)
1,000 people, 1995				
Constant	–1.39***	–1.75***	–1.66***	–1.65***
R-Square	.610	.612	.670	.696
N	74	74	74	66

[#]Self-expression values: WVS, 1995–2000. The five variables that make up the self-expression factors include: tolerance of human diversity (V208, tolerance of homosexuality), rejecting paternalism (V13, one should respect parents unconditionally-rejection); progender equality (V78 men have more rights to jobs than women-rejection), liberty aspiration (calculated from V120-124 concerning respondent's view of national priorities), and importance of leisure (V6). For countries surveyed in 2000, the 2000 data is used; for others (about 10 cases), the 1995 data is used.

[a]In thousands, World Bank Development Report.

[b, c]Both rounded to the closest percentile (meaning, <5% = 0, 6–15% = 1, 26–35% = 3, etc.), World Bank Development Report.

*α<.05; **α<.01; ***α<.001.

East Asia in Generations: 1930s–1990s

As displayed previously, while the data have allowed us to see some clear upward trend in South Korea and Japan from 1981 to 2000, we have only fragmentary evidence.[4] On the other hand, because we have fairly good data collected from all six societies during the 1999–2001 wave,[5] a look into different generations in these societies will allow us to see how social values have changed in the last several decades.

Figure 4.3 shows a clear increase in self-expression values in these societies during the last six generations or so, with each generation of a society plotted. Years marked on the x-axis are the years between which each generation is between 10 to 20 years old. In other words, the third cohort from the left was 10 to 20 years old between 1956 and 1965 (i.e., the cohort born between 1946 and 1955). We look at the period between 10 to 20 years old because that period comprises an individual's formative age. Their social values usually form during this time, and once formed, their values stay stable through their adult years.

This chart shows most notably that Korea and Japan see consistent and continuous increase in self-expression values from older to younger cohorts. We have witnessed similar intergenerational value shifts in other societies. This finding reveals several significant things. First, except for Japan, these societies all started at about the same level of self-expression values, as shown by the position of the cohorts that grew up before 1945. This suggests two things: 1) that Japan's socioeconomic development was already much higher than the others before the end of World War II, resulting in the fact that its population was already higher in terms of self-expression values; and 2) that all the other societies had very similar social values before industrialization.

Second, once rapid industrialization takes place, people's values shift toward more emphasis on self-expression. Indeed, Japan, regardless of its higher starting point, witnessed continuous increase in self-expression values in the postwar period as industrialization and postindustrialization in that country occurred rapidly. The three newly industrialized countries

Figure 4.3. Intergenerational value shifts in six Confucian societies.

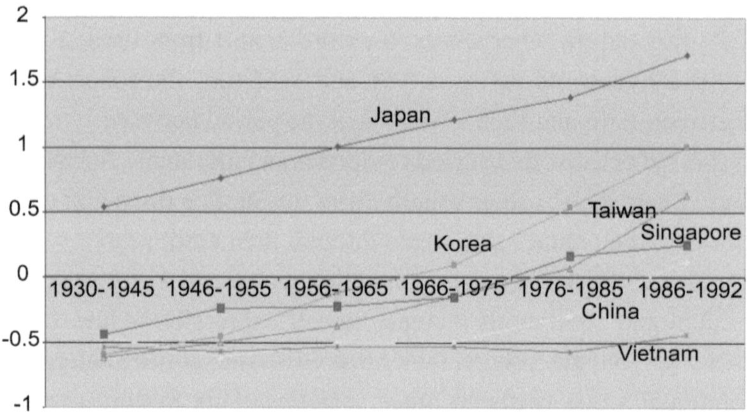

Source. 1999–2001 WVS of Japan, Korea, Singapore, China, and Vietnam, 1995 WVS of Taiwan.
The numbers on the X axis show the years during which each cohort is between 10–20 years old.
Self-expression values: A factor score of six variables: liberty aspiration, tolerance, gender equality, attitude toward patriarchal family relationships, attitude toward paternalism at the workplace, and importance of leisure.

(NIC), Korea, Taiwan, and Singapore, also manifested significant gains in self-expression values once their economies took off in 1960s.[6] Indeed, in all three societies, we see a clear leap from the 1946–1955 cohort to the 1956–1965 cohort. And after that, the increase between the younger cohort and older cohort was even faster, as the slope of each of the lines becomes steeper. To some extent, it looks like Korea is moving toward a convergence with Japan, so is Taiwan to a lesser extent. Such a convergence may well happen in the coming decades as both Korea and Taiwan enjoy a sufficiently long postindustrial stage of development.

Third, such a thesis (i.e., value change toward self-expression caused by economic growth, industrialization, and postindustrialization) gets further vindication from China and Vietnam. Neither country witnessed significant changes of value between cohorts until the 1980s for China and the 1990s for Vietnam. We can explain this almost perfectly by the history of economic growth and modernization in these two countries. In China, rapid economic growth and modernization started at the beginning of the 1980s, as the reformists within the CCP (headed by Deng Xiaoping) set the country to the course in 1978. Since then, the economy has grown between 7% and 12% each year for more than 20 years, and material security has greatly improved. As a result, the youngest two cohorts in China show significantly higher level of self-expression values compared to earlier cohorts. Vietnam has a similar situation. The Vietnamese economy picked up some fast growth in the late 1980s and early 1990s as the regime started a program of economic reform similar to that of China. As a result, self-expression values have increased among the Vietnamese public, but only in recent years.

Thus, in hindsight, decades of economic growth and industrialization do give rise in these societies to a public more and more liberty oriented, outspoken, tolerant, and proequality (between genders, within family, and in the workplace). This goes back to our familiar argument about the economic wealth of a nation and the level of democracy.[7] Economic growth is conducive to the emergence and quality of democracy not because (or not mainly because) it gives people more food, better housing, and more money to spend on luxury goods. It brings a host of social changes generally known as modernization. Economic growth, industrialization, and modernization give rise to a public that emphasizes liberty and participation in government, among others. Through this linkage people in these changing societies advance democracy.[8]

Self-Expression Values and Democracy

The main idea of the self-expression values argument is that economic growth brings material security, enabling people to shift their priorities from survival and physical needs to psychological needs, that is, to pursue a sense of belonging, empowerment, and self-realization. It is no accident that studies of European politics first revealed such findings (Gibbins, 1989; Inglehart, 1977, 1990), as industrialization and postindustrialization first took place and held on in Europe (excluding North America). Following Europe's lead, East Asia's NICs take a similar path. Into the 21st century, NICs will include China, India, Vietnam, and Malaysia. Thus, we should expect to see the rise of self-expression values in these places in the 21st century, as indeed we have already witnessed in China and Vietnam (Figure 4.3).

The real intellectual puzzle now arises. Why is the rise of self-expression values related to the rise of democracy? We know that countries with higher self-expression values during the 1990s have made more progress in democratization (Welzel, Inglehart, & Klingemann, 2003). Indeed, of the six societies under examination here, the relationship seems clear. Table 4.5 shows that the higher a country's self-expression score, the more democratic its political system, as measured by the Freedom House democracy rating.

Of course, this table shows only limited evidence supports the argument that the rise of self-expression values will lead to the improvement of democratic governance in a given society. Above all, it includes only six cases. In the following chapters I will examine this relationship with empirical data. I will show how the rise of self-expression values has affected citizen politics and answer the questions: is a self-expression-oriented person more likely to participate in activities pressuring the government for accountability and responsiveness, such as protesting or demonstrating (chapter 6)? Is a self-expression-oriented person more critical toward government institutions (chapter 8)? Both these behaviors on the part of citizens will likely make the government more democratic. Is a self-expression-oriented person more active in social and civic organizations, thus creating more social capital (chapter 7)? Higher social capital makes democratic institutions function better, as generally believed now. Thus, on the one hand social capital helps increase the quality of democracy in a democratic society and on the other hand prepares citizens for upcoming democratic institutions in societies not yet democratized. With these questions answered, we should come to an understanding of the linkage of self-expression and democracy.

Table 4.5. Mean self-expression scores and Freedom House ratings.

Country	*Self-Expression Score (2000)*	*Freedom House Democracy Rating 1990–1999 (Reversed)*
Japan	1.069978	109
Korea	0.219726	97
Taiwan	–0.17649[a]	86
Singapore	0.011192	46
China	–0.39665	2
Vietnam	–0.53343	0

Source. Self-expression score: Calculated by the author based on data from WVS 1999–2001 (except for Taiwan); Freedom House rating: Freedom House Inc. (www.freedomhouse.org)
Self-expression score: National mean of a factor score including six attitudes: liberty aspiration, tolerance, against patriarchy, against paternalism, pro gender equality, and emphasizing leisure in life.
Freedom House rating: Freedom House rates each country every year by 1 to 7 in two dimensions: civil liberty and political rights. The lower the score, the freer a country. The numbers in this table are calculated by first adding up the rating of each country of every year from 1990 to 1999 (the highest score one country can get in a certain year is 14, and 2 the lowest). The sum score is reversed so that the scores of the more democratic countries are higher than that of the less democratic.
[a]1995 data.

NOTES

1. In China's 2001 Survey, 97% of those answering chose yes to the question "Are you willing to fight in a war for this country?" The percentage in Vietnam was 98, Singapore 87, Taiwan 87, South Korea 75, and Japan 25.
2. One can further postulate that if there were survey data from North Korea, the percentage of North Korean people willing to fight in a war would be very high, given the regime's extremely intense indoctrination.
3. Factor analysis uses listwise elimination of missing variables. As a result, the sample of the 1990 Japanese survey, when a factor of five variables is created, has only about 600 valid cases. Because the 2000 survey has about 1,300 valid cases, the factor scores for the cases in the 2000 sample are disproportionately large.
4. While we also have survey data for three waves from China (1990, 1995, and 2000), the samples from 1990 and 1995 are not comparable to that of 2000, which is the highest quality. Because of this, a cross-wave comparison of China's data is not used.
5. Except for Taiwan, for which we use one wave of data collected in 1995.
6. For studies of East Asian industrialization experiences, see Haggard, 1990; Johnson, 1982.
7. See discussions by, among others, Lipset (1959), and Prwzeski (Przeworski, Alvarez, Cheibub, & Limongi, 2000; Przeworski & Limongi, 1997).
8. Indeed, without such a complex process of social changes and modernization, a wealthy country will not necessarily become a democracy. Scholars have tested and confirmed this thesis regarding the lack of democracy in oil-rich, oil-producing countries (Ross, 2001).

Chapter 5

Education and Self-Expression Values: Socioeconomic and Psychological Paths

This chapter examines the role of education in affecting value changes of citizens in East Asian society. That education shapes an individual's values is not in question, and the importance of education in producing democratic citizens cannot be overstressed. Classical writers such as Almond and Verba (1963) and Jennings (Jennings & Niemi, 1974) have pointed to such important links between education and democratic attitudes. Nevertheless, some questions still draw debate regarding how education matters to an individual's social and political attitudes. For example, does education make a democratic citizen by shaping the disposition and value system of the individual, or does education simply position an individual in social settings conducive to the forming of democratic attitudes (e.g., enabling an individual to assume a white-collar job)? The first path we can call a psychological, cognitive, pedagogical, or epistemological path, while the second we can call a socioeconomic one.

Such questions have not been thoroughly examined with hard data in East Asian societies. This chapter attempts to move in this direction and focuses on the impact of education on the rise of self-expression values. In examining the role of education, I will emphasize higher education (i.e., postsecondary or college education and beyond). Indeed, the effect of education on democratic attitudes has been more carefully studied in democratic societies; under authoritarian regimes the question of whether education can lead to similarly prodemocratic attitudes has not received a clear answer. Above all, authoritarian regimes tend to control the process and content of education and often use education as part of the state effort to indoctrinate citizens into values conducive to regime sustainability. My angle here is a little different. Self-expression values do not relate directly to regime loyalty or respect of the political system. They are the latent desire for freedom, liberty, and rights. If our data show that education makes citizens more self-expression oriented, then despite state control of education, the demand for democracy will rise with a rising level of public education. If, however, data show that an individual's level of education does not affect self-expression orientation (especially in societies where an authoritarian state controls education), then we will need to reconsider the role of education in promoting democratic citizens.

Education in Modernization and Postmodernization

If modernization means the process of economic growth and industrialization, no doubt the spread of mass education is one integral part of it. Most directly, education supplies human capital that makes industrialization and economic growth possible. Today the scholarly debate in development economics is not about the importance of education or human capital but rather how to spend resources on education to achieve the maximum return in economic growth (Blankenau & Simpson, 2004; Temple, 1999). In the later stage of industrialization (the postindustrialization stage), rise of the knowledge sector means an increasing need for a workforce with a higher education. If we agree that wealth and affluence result from modernization, and postmodernization contributes to the rise of self-expression values, then we can say that rising mass education contributes to rising self-expression values, as education may be considered a cause of modernization and postmodernization.

Modernization is not merely about the growth of wealth, however, but also about social changes, and education has a role in this, too. For example, changes in the occupational structure of a society will expose individuals to a higher level of social complexity. At the basic level, modernization requires labor moving from agrarian to manufacturing and service sectors, and increasing mass education and higher education is a prerequisite for such structural changes to take place. Such changes, no doubt, have tremendous impact on social values. In fact, Nobel Prize-winning economist Sen has emphatically argued that an increase in women's education is the most important reason for the decline in the fertility rate in several Indian regions (Sen, 1999), reflecting significant changes in family and social values. The new social roles educated women acquire in industrial and postindustrial society represent a main reason for the changes related to gender attitudes at the societal level (Inglehart & Norris, 2003). In any case, one may hypothesize that, if education has an impact on self-expression values, this impact takes place by placing people in a different mode of existence.

Education has a role not only because it places individuals in a certain occupational position or puts them in a world where individuals encounter a much higher level of social complexity. It also has a more direct role: it enables people to generate and consume mass information. With modern education comes mass consumption of information, a social change that can have a direct impact on politics (Deutsch, 1961).

To sum up, three paths exist through which education contributes to value changes, more specifically to the rise of self-expression values: (1) by increasing affluence; (2) by mobilizing workforces into modern sectors, such as manufacturing and service industries; and (3) by immersing individuals in mass information and communication. This categorization allows us to test the effects of education on self-expression values through statistical analyses. Here I test these hypotheses:

1. Education has a positive impact on self-expression values; such an impact, however, can be partially accounted for by

2. level of wealth;
3. occupational structures of a society; and
4. the degree of mass information.

Testing Modernization Theory

I tested the aforementioned hypotheses using value data collected from WVS and socioeconomic development data released by the World Bank. Countries or societies for which we have at least one wave of WVS data comprise the units of analysis. The following are variables included in the analyses.

Dependent variable: Self-expression values, a factor score that includes several value dimensions: liberty aspiration, tolerance, personal happiness, gender equality attitude, and rejection of paternalism. This measurement of self-expression values has been used throughout this study; however, it is calculated at the level of nations, not individuals.

Independent variables follow.

Education and Higher Education. I use two variables to measure the level of education in each country. For mass education, I use percentage of female age cohort in secondary education. Scholars of development have long considered this a strong indicator of access to mass education in a country. Intuitively, people refer to adult literacy rate as the indicator of a society's level of mass education. But for many countries, especially advanced industrial countries, literacy rate offers a less useful indicator, as every country has a literacy rate of almost 100%. Hence using percentage of female children in school offers a much more effective indicator.

A second measurement of education I use in this analysis, the gross college enrollment rate, equals the percentage of age cohort enrolled in college. This creates a measurement of the access to higher education in a society.

Gross National Income (GNI) Per Capita measures the level of material wealth. Following international standards, I use a purchasing power parity figure, generally considered a more accurate measurement of wealth than exchange rate parity figures.

Occupational Structure is measured by two variables: percentage of labor force in manufacturing jobs and percentage of labor force in the service industry. The first variable measures the degree of industrialization, while the second one measures the degree of postindustrialization.

Mass Information is also measured by two variables. Traditionally, in the stage of industrialization, the rise of newspapers indicates the spread of mass information. Thus, number of daily newspapers consumed by, say, 1,000 people is a good indicator of how much inroads traditional media have made into the society. In postindustrial societies, mass information spreads by electronic media, such as radio, TV, movies, and more and more so by telephone, fax, cellular phones, and the Internet. Thus, I use the number of personal computers owned by 1,000 people as an indicator of the usage of information in the postindustrial and knowledge society.

For all these independent variables, I intend to identify the causal direction by careful temporal selections. That is to say, while I use the strength of self-expression values of a certain society at around 2000 as the dependent variable (mostly surveyed in the 1999–2001 wave), I use all the socioeconomic indicators (independent variables) of around 1995. Thus, we can be relatively confident that socioeconomic variables cause variations on the dependent variable.

As I have discussed, my theoretical framework would lead us to expect two major findings. First, education will have a positive and strong impact on self-expression values. Second, however, because education has such an effect through the three paths I identified earlier, once we introduce the variables of socioeconomic modernization (wealth, occupational structure, and information), we should the effect of education on self-expression values to decrease. That is, such socioeconomic variables will account for a portion of education's impact on self-expression values.

Modernization: Empirical Evidence

Tables 5.1, 5.2, and 5.3 contain the empirical results. From Model 5-1 through Model 5-6, I in turn introduced the variables of mass education, GNI per capita, and other socioeconomic indicators (Table 5.1). From Model 5-7 through Model 5-12, I repeated the same tests, but replaced mass education with higher education–gross enrollment in colleges (Table 5.2). Model 5-13 and Model 5-14 include both mass education and higher education (Table 5.3).

These findings confirm what I expected. First, mass education and higher education both have a positive and significant effect on the strength of self-expression values of a certain society (Model 5-1). Second, however, such effects decrease significantly once the socioeconomic variables are introduced, as shown by Models 5-2 through 5-6, and 5-7 through 5-12. Specifically, once we introduce wealth (GNI), postindustrialization (proportion of labor force in service), and information (number of computers per thousand people), the effect of education stops being statistically significant (Models 5-5, 5-6, and 5-12). Lastly, some of the socioeconomic variables are consistently

Table 5.1. Education and self-expression values.

Dependent Variable: Strength of Self-Expression Values Around 2000[#]			
	Standardized Beta		
	Model 5-1	*Model 5-2*	*Model 5-3*
Percentage of female age cohort enrolled in secondary education, about 1995	.635****	.173*	.187*
GNI per capita 1995[a]		.713****	.712****
Percentage of labor force in industry 1995[b]			–.021
Percentage of labor force in service sector 1995[c]			
Daily newspapers per 1,000 people, 1995			
Personal computers per 1,000 people, 1999			
R-Square	.403	.698	.698
N	65	64	64
	Model 5-4	*Model 5-5*	*Model 5-6*
Percentage female age cohort enrolled in secondary education, about 1995	.096	.037	.089
GNI per capita 1995[a]	.606****	.544****	.331**
Percentage of labor force in industry 1995[b]	–.028		

Percentage of labor force in service sector 1995[c]	.275***	.244**	.238**
Daily newspaper per 1000 people, 1995		.144	
Personal computers per 1,000 people, 1999			.314*
R-Square	.740	.730	.756
N	64	60	55

[#]Self-expression values: WVS, 1995–2000. The five variables that make up the self-expression factor are: tolerance of human diversity (V208, tolerance of homosexuality), rejecting paternalism (V13, one should respect one's parents unconditionally-rejection); progender equality (V78, men have more right to jobs than women-rejection), liberty aspiration (calculated from V120-124, concerning respondent's view of national priorities), and importance of leisure (V6). For countries surveyed in 2000, the 2000 data is used; for others (about 10 cases), the 1995 data is used.

[a]In thousands, World Bank Development Report.

[b, c]Both rounded to the closest percentile (meaning, <5% = 0, 6–15% = 1, 26–35% = 3, etc.), World Bank Development Report.

$*\alpha<.10$; $**\alpha<.05$; $***\alpha\leq.01$; $****\alpha<.001$.

Table 5.2. Higher education and self-expression values.

Dependent Variable: Strength of Self-Expression Values Around 2000[#]			
		Standardized Beta	
	Model 5-7	*Model 5-8*	*Model 5-9*
Percentage age cohort enrolled in colleges, about 1995	.647****	.319***	.263***
GNI per capita 1995[a]		.580****	.601****
Percentage of labor force in industry 1995[b]			.072
Percentage of labor force in service sector 1995[c]			
Daily newspapers per 1,000 people, 1995			
Personal computers per 1,000 people, 1999			
R-Square	.419	.680	.690
N	77	73	71
	Model 5-10	*Model 5-11*	*Model 5-12*
Percentage age cohort enrolled in colleges, about 1995	.193*	.193**	0
GNI per capita 1995[a]	.523****	.383***	.364*
Percentage of labor force in industry 1995[b]	–.059		
Percentage of labor force in service sector 1995[c]	.204***	.189**	.228**
Daily newspapers per 1,000 people, 1995		.225**	

Personal computers per 1,000 people, 1999			.341*
R-Square	.712	.715	.731
N	71	66	57

[#]Self-expression values: WVS, 1995–2000. The five variables that make up the self-expression factor are: tolerance of human diversity (V208, tolerance of homosexuality), rejecting paternalism (V13, one should respect one's parents unconditionally-rejection); progender equality (V78, men have more right to jobs than women-rejection), liberty aspiration (calculated from V120-124, concerning respondent's view of national priorities), and importance of leisure (V6). For countries surveyed in 2000, the 2000 data is used; for others (about 10 cases), the 1995 data is used.

[a]In thousands, World Bank Development Report.

[b, c]Both rounded to the closest percentile (meaning, <5% = 0, 6–15% = 1, 26–35% = 3, etc.), World Bank Development Report.

*α<.10; **α<.05; ***$\alpha\leq$.01; ****α<.001

Table 5.3. Education, higher education, and self-expression values.

Dependent Variable: Strength of Self-Expression Values Around 2000[#]	*Standardized Beta*			
	Model 5-1	*Model 5-7*	*Model 5-13*	*Model 5-14*
Percentage female age cohort enrolled in secondary education, about 1995	.635****		.221*	.132
Percentage age cohort enrolled in colleges, about 1995		.647****	.552****	–.145
GNI per capita 1995[a]				.377**
Percentage of labor force in industry1995[b]				
Percentage of labor force in service sector 1995[c]				.260***
Daily newspapers per 1,000 people, 1995				
Personal computers per 1,000 people, 1999				.345*
R-Square	.403	.419	.536	.761
N	65	77	65	55

[#]Self-expression values: WVS, 1995–2000. The five variables that make up the self-expression factor are: tolerance of human diversity (V208, tolerance of homosexuality), rejecting paternalism (V13, one should respect one's parents unconditionally-rejection); progender equality (V78, men have more right to jobs than women-rejection), liberty aspiration (calculated from V120-124, concerning respondent's view of national priorities), and importance of leisure (V6). For countries surveyed in 2000, the 2000 data is used; for others (about 10 cases), the 1995 data is used.

[a]In thousands, World Bank Development Report.

[b, c]Both rounded to the closest percentile (meaning, $<5\% = 0$, $6–15\% = 1$, $26–35\% = 3$, etc.), World Bank Development Report.

$^{*}\alpha<.10$; $^{**}\alpha<.05$; $^{***}\alpha\leq.01$; $^{****}\alpha<.001$

significant: wealth, percentage of labor force in service sector, and number of computers per thousand people. These variables largely account for the effect of education on self-expression. This seems to support the earlier theoretical argument that rising self-expression values is an outcome of affluence, postindustrialization, and the arrival of a knowledge society (Inglehart, 1990; Inglehart & Baker, 2000), but it also shows that education affects value changes directly through socioeconomic paths.

Democracy's Contribution

The above analyses show that education represents an important factor contributing to the growth of self-expression values. Although we know education affects the growth of self-expression values through socioeconomic paths, such as by increasing the proportion of a population engaged in the service industry and by enabling more people to consume information (such as the use of computers and other information technologies), we did not examine a political variable. That is, does education play a stronger role in a democratic vis-à-vis in a nondemocratic society? We can test this proposition using global data by specifically looking at the intervening effect. If we find that in countries with a higher degree of democracy, the effects of education on individual level of self-expression values is stronger, then we can say that, where democracy is better developed, education plays a stronger role in promoting self-expression values. In this sense, democratic institutions and self-expression values may have a mutually enhancing effect: the growth of one will improve the other, a virtuous circle of a sort.

We can accomplish this by using a multilevel regression method.[1] Among the 60-odd societies for which we have the latest WVS data, the degree of democracy for each country varies. We can look at the effects of education on self-expression values at different degrees of democracy of an individual country. Table 5.4 presents this test. Model 1 shows the level-1 effect of education on self-expression values on the individual level with the pooled data set. Cleary, higher attainment in education can translate into stronger self-expression values. In Model 2, I add a country's degree of democracy, calculated as the sum of a country's Freedom House results for the 10 years before the survey (sum of reversed Freedom House score of a country from 1991 through 2000). This level-2 variable shows that if a country is more democratic, the people within the country tend to hold stronger self-expression values. In the third model, I add another term specifying the interaction between a country's degree of democracy and an individual's level of education, denoted as Education Level multiplied by Degree of Democracy in the table. This allows the effect of education on self-expression values to vary with a country's level of democracy. As the results show, this term is significant and positive, indicating that in countries with stronger democratic institutions, education tends to have a stronger effect on the growth of self-expression values. Hence, it does appear that between democracy and self-expression values there exists a virtuous circle; the effect of education on self-expression values increases with rising levels of democracy, while rising self-expression values also contribute to improvement of democratic institutions.

To add a caveat, in the next step I control the interaction of democracy with education for the interaction of economic development with education. In Model 4, I added the interaction term, denoted as Education Level multiplied by Economic Development

Table 5.4. Democracy's contribution to education's effects on self-expression values.

Dependent Variable: Self-Expression Values, About 2000				
Fixed Effects	*Model 1*	*Model 2*	*Model 3*	*Model 4*
Intercept	–.545719	–1.125640	–1.106539	–1.068102
	(.070565)***	(.170974)***	(.170415)***	(.177885)***
Education level	.085475	.085592	.050786	.032356
	(.005937)***	(.006187)***	(.011222)***	(.007866)***
Degree of democracy of country		.007031	.006787	.006483
		(.001979)**	(.001973)**	(.002061)**
Education level*			.000436	.000240
Degree of democracy (1991–2000)			(.000154)**	(.000144)[a]
Education level*				.0000050
Economic development				(.0000013)***
Random Effects	*Model 1*	*Model 2*	*Model 3*	*Model 4*
Intercept	.305529	.258614	.256652	.262718
	(.056437)***	(.049699)***	(.049331)***	(.053352)***
Education level	.002034	.002110	.000638	
	(.000406)***	(.000430)***	(.000319)***	Redundant
Education level*			.00000016	

Degree of democracy			(.00000006)*	Redundant
Education level*				
Economic development				Redundant
Residual	.633149 (.003584)***	.630448 (.003626)***	.630453 (.003626)***	.628732 (.003659)***
Model Fit Statistics	*Model 1*	*Model 2*	*Model 3*	*Model 4*
-2 Restricted log likelihood	149487.4	144537.0	144538.7	140940.2
AIC	149493.4	144543.0	144546.7	140950.2
BIC	149520.6	144570.0	144582.8	140995.2

Source. WVS Global Dataset, Fourth Wave (around 2000).
Note. Education level: WVS code from 1 to 10.
Degree of democracy: Sum of a given country's Freedom House score from 1991 through 2000, reversed so that the higher the score, the higher the degree of democracy.
Economic development: GDP per capita in purchasing power parity dollars as of 1995 for any given country.
$^{*}\alpha < .05$; $^{**}\alpha < .01$; $^{***}\alpha < .001$; $^{a}\alpha < .10$

(measured by a country's GDP per capita as of 1995). This will indicate, after controlling the impact of modernization, whether democracy still affects education's role in promoting self-expression values. As it turns out, once we control the level of modernization, the effect of democracy on the role of education decreases by almost one half, from .000436 to .000240, and this effect almost ceases to be significant (it is significant only at the .10 level). This message might be encouraging. As long as modernization takes place, education will continue to promote self-expression values even if the society is not yet a democracy. In other words, even under nondemocratic regimes, a rising level of education will give rise to self-expression values, which in the end will help usher in democracy.

EDUCATION AS A TRANSFORMING PROCESS

Scholars have found education changes citizen's political attitudes and behaviors in two ways. First, it shapes people's values and attitudes as they develop toward adulthood. Second, education places people in a higher social strata, and people in different social positions adopt different behavioral patterns related to political involvement (Nie, Junn, & Stehlik-Barry, 1996). At the individual level, no study examined education's impact on self-expression values. Nonetheless, we do have a rich literature on how education contributes to democratic citizenship. Basically, we understand education (and higher education) as a transforming process for individuals. Such transformative effects occur in two ways. First, education is a process in which ideological and attitudinal teachings take place; second, education is an experience that develops and defines an individual's value system.

This understanding parallels two kinds of educational thinking in preparing competent citizens for democracy. One, design and implement curricular programs with the goal to promote civic learning; transmit civic knowledge to students through various pedagogical methods—the instructional approach. The other approach holds that student growth, including progress toward democratic outcomes, is affected by the broader school or college experience, while formal instruction is just one of the ways. This line of thinking tends to look at a student's college experience from a more holistic view, and can be termed as the experiential-learning approach.

Teaching Civic Values

The original meaning of democratic or civic education, say the study of political knowledge, includes knowledge of democracy, government and politics, and citizenship (Branson & Quigley, 1998; Galston, 2001). The other elements of democratic citizenship, such as civic values, will naturally grow following the acquirement of relevant knowledge. For example, the more one knows about politics, the more one understands the effect of public policies, thus the more likely one will participate in political processes (Delli Carpini & Keeter, 1996). For another example, the more one knows about political principles and institutions, the more one likely will support democratic principles, such as tolerance. Nie et al. (1996) find a direct relationship between knowledge of democratic principles and tolerance. In fact, Galston (2001) points out seven ways in which basic civic information is linked to civic attitudes (pp. 223–224).

Civic education comes, probably more effectively, through a liberal education curriculum in higher education. Liberal education in higher education has long been linked to the ideal of democracy and the relationship between individuals and the polity. Liberal education emphasizes the study of the humanities, including the most important political and philosophical thoughts developed during the history of human civilization. It aims at leading individuals to examine critically the existence of humanity as individuals and as communities of different sizes and kinds (Bloom, 1990). Thus imagined, liberal education plays an important formative role in preparing members for a democratic community.

This civic function of college education largely represents the connection between education and self-expression values. Self-expression values emphasize individual liberty and political rights; they embrace open, equal, and tolerant social and political relations. Clearly, a liberal education program will direct the individual toward such intellectual transformation. Another way to think about this is that, self-expression values in many ways overlap with other value conceptions, such as individual modernity (Inkeles, 1966), liberal values (Flanagan & Lee, 2000), or similar various conceptions of modern values. Then, the liberal education curriculum as an important intellectual descendant of the Enlightenment, certainly aims at promoting such values and beliefs.

Thus, we should expect to find that, individuals with a college education should demonstrate stronger self-expression values than those without one. But we base such an expectation on the assumption that the liberal education curriculum, or at least a major part of it, is immersed in the college education. This might create a problematic assumption for countries outside the Anglo–Saxon influence. Above all, what we generally call liberal education is largely made up of the cannons in the American (or Western) intellectual tradition. If the college curriculum of, say, a Confucian society or a Communist society does not adopt such values, can we still expect such an effect of a college education on self-expression values?

In fact, education affects an individual's values not only or not mainly through the classroom instruction she receives. Education as a transforming process takes place more through the school experience, a large part of which lies outside the classroom and curricular activities. Extracurricular experiences tend to promote self-expression values, regardless of how curriculum materials are defined. Hence, our understanding of the impact of education (and college education in particular) should focus more on how college experiences as a whole affect an individual's prodemocratic outlooks. This perspective requires us first to focus on the interaction between an individual learner (the student) and the environment in which learning takes place; and second to put an emphasis on the various learning experiences, especially those occurring outside formal classroom teaching.

Education scholars have produced tremendous research that supports these two linkages. Generally, a college education transforms a student's values by

1. involvement in college, such as participation in campus activities, student organizations, leadership programs, art and cultural events, and interaction with faculty, staff, and peers (Astin, 1984; Kuh, 1991; Pascarella & Terenzini, 1991);
2. community service and service learning (Astin & Sax, 1998); and

3. encounters with diversity, that is, students have more chances to work with peers and other socialization agents with different backgrounds, perspectives, and ideas (Schoem & Hurtado, 2001).

Such an emphasis on education as a socialization process parallels the sociological literature that explains the rise of postmaterialism and modern and postmodern values emphasizing the different features of the (post-) industrial societal environment in which individuals live their existences: information, cognitive mobilization, and encounters with social complexities (Inglehart, 1990; Misztal, 1996). In any case, we can test the effect of education and college experience on self-expression values at the individual level.

Psychological Paths: Empirical Evidences

To test this hypothesis in the six Confucian societies for which we have survey data, I run regressions for each country, using individual education as the main explanatory variable. I should first note that this data does not provide information enabling us to look into the educational process itself. Thus, we cannot sort out the effect of different components of the educational experience as specified by educational researchers. For example, we cannot assess the impact of formal curricular activities, extracurricular involvement, or quality of effort, on the development of self-expression values. But we should be comfortable with this, as long as our research design allows us to assess the effect of education as a whole unit of an individual's developmental process. Above all, more focused research efforts of scholars have proved that the different components of the educational experience have different effects on value development. At our level of abstraction, we should be content to leave out those intricacies.

Furthermore, the role of education as a transforming process or institution for individuals holds more interest for us. We know that education also serves as a placement process or institution, that is, as scholars argue, education places people into different social strata (Nie, Junn, & Stehlik-Barry, 1996). To account for this placement effect of education, I include in the controlling variables the socioeconomic background of individuals, such as financial status, life satisfaction, professional background, and size of town one lives in. To account for education's effect on cognitive mobilization, I include one's interest in politics as a controlling variable.

I introduce education in two separate ways: as measured by the number of years of formal education and as a dichotomous measurement according to whether or not one receives a college education. Besides the controlling variables I described above, as a general rule, demographic variables such as gender, age, and marital status are also controlled. I also control religiosity. As a major component of the traditional–rational dimension of value change in modernizing societies, it can control the traditionalism of one's belief system. Table 5.5 presents the findings in an abridged form.

I have organized Table 5.5 in two panels. The upper panel reports the findings of democratic societies in East Asia: South Korea, Taiwan, and Japan, while the lower panel reports the nondemocratic ones: Singapore, Vietnam, and China. I have in fact found no significantly different findings across these societies, and this organization is only for the purpose of convenience. We can clearly say that education level of an individual

Table 5.5. Impact of education and higher education on self-expression values.

Dependent Variable: Individual-Level Self-Expression Values						
	South Korea		*Taiwan*		*Japan*	
Democratic Confucian Asia	*Model I*	*Model II*	*Model I*	*Model II*	*Model I*	*Model II*
Years of formal education	.078***		.047***		.029*	
	(.009)		(.010)		(.012)	
Higher education (dichotomous)		.295***		.445***		.197*
		(.053)		(.093)		(.085)
R-Square	.301	.282	.205	.201	.214	.203
N	1,415		962		719	
	Singapore		*Vietnam*		*China*	
Nondemocratic Confucian Asia	*Model I*	*Model II*	*Model I*	*Model II*	*Model I*	*Model II*
Years of formal education	.019*		.047***		.048***	
	(.007)		(.009)		(.010)	
Higher education (dichotomous)		.350***		.328**		.385**
		(.087)		(.114)		(.140)
R-Square	.201	.214	.085	.069	.164	.153
N	1,364		1,161		1,114	
All models controlling	age, gender, marital status, interest in politics, religiosity (importance of God), financial situations, life satisfaction, size of town (where applicable), and professional background					

Source. WVS, 2000.
$*\alpha<.05$; $**\alpha<.01$; $***\alpha<.001$

does translate into higher self-expression values. In each society, each additional year of formal education means a difference of self-expression values ranging from 0.02 unit (Singapore) to 0.08 unit (South Korea). Thus, on average, a person with 12 years of formal education will demonstrate a self-expression values strength between 0.24 unit (in Singapore) and 0.96 unit (in South Korea) higher, compared to a person with no formal education. That is, the difference may range from one quarter to one full standard deviation.

If we look at the impact of college education, we can see that on average, college education makes a difference in self-expression values ranging from 0.2 (Japan) to 0.45 (Taiwan).

Does College Make a *Big* Difference?

Besides that education in general and college education in particular, make a difference in people's self-expression values, these findings reveal a more complex message. Basically we see that the difference made by a college education cannot simply be accounted for by the mere number of years of education. That is, simply counting college as an additional 2 or 4 years of education beyond the precollege period does not explain the big difference it makes. This should not surprise us given that the literature points to important ways through which college affects value changes, which are not available or much limited in an elementary and secondary education environment.

One rough calculation will drive this message home. First, we can estimate that in our sample, those coded as college educated on average have 15 years of formal education. Given that about half of these people received a 2-year college degree, using 15 as the average years of education should not be very problematic. Second, we estimate that in our sample, those with no college education average 10 years of education. This number might be low for countries such as Japan and South Korea, where K–12 education is almost universal. But it may be high for China and Vietnam, where the national goal for universal education is a 9-year basic education. Nonetheless, we can proceed with this 15-10 combination, and make adjustments if necessary. (See Table 5.6)

Table 5.6 presents the idea of how such a comparison works and the results of such a comparison. D_1 and D_2 are merely copied from Table 5.5. D_1 stands for the difference made by each year of formal education, while D_2 stands for the difference between people with a college education and people without. Thus, 15 and 10 years of formal education should make a difference in self-expression values of D_1*15 and D_1*10, respectively, presented as S_1 and S_2 in the table. To find out whether a college education has a bigger impact than merely as an accumulation of years of formal education, we simply need to find out whether the difference between S_1 and S_2 is greater than D_2.

The difference between S_1 and S_2 is presented as D_3. As it turns out, in every country except in South Korea, D_3 is smaller than D_2. That is, the difference made by a college education is indeed bigger than the difference made by 5 more years of formal education.[2] Thus, the calculation has confirmed that a college education makes a difference greater than merely an addition of several years of formal education. College education does have the sociopsychological effect on self-expression values that a precollege education does not have.

Table 5.6. Difference in self-expression values made by a college education compared with education in general.

			Difference made by a college education if merely treated as another 4 years of formal education			
			D_3			
	Difference made by 1 year of formal education	*Difference made by a college education*	*Difference made by 15 years of education*	*Difference made by 10 years of education*	*Difference made by 15 vs. 10 years of education*	*Is difference made by a real college education greater?*
Country	D_1	D_2	$S_1 = D_1 * 15$	$S_2 = D_1 * 10$	$D_3 = S_1 - S_2$	$D_2 - D_3 >= 0?$
South Korea	.078	.295	1.17	0.78	0.39	–0.095
Taiwan	.047	.445	0.705	0.47	0.235	0.21
Japan	.029	.197	0.435	0.29	0.145	0.052
Singapore	.019	.350	0.285	0.19	0.095	0.255
Vietnam	.047	.328	0.705	0.47	0.235	0.093
China	.048	.385	0.72	0.48	0.24	0.145

Source. Calculated from Table 5.5.

CONCLUSION

I have examined the impact of education in general, and higher education in particular, on the forming of self-expression values. I have done this on two levels of analysis: societal level and individual level. On the societal level, I refer to literature on modernization and postmodernization as a societal process, with which come changes in social life and social values. In this process, education contributes to value changes, more specifically to the rise of self-expression values through three paths:

1. education, with its functions in increasing literacy and technological advancement of economic production, help increases societal wealth;
2. education reallocates workforces into modern sectors (basically manufacturing and service); and
3. education makes mass information consumption possible.

To be sure, these paths may not be conclusive, and certainly they are not mutually exclusive. But to the extent that we can sort them out, my empirical tests have proved the existence of these paths through which education contributes to the rise of self-expression values—the socioeconomic paths.

On the individual level, I look into the literature on how education, especially college education, changes people's values toward more democratically oriented ways. With the solid support of this literature, I hypothesize that people with a college education should be more self-expression oriented than others. The individual level analysis has confirmed this hypothesis. Education, then, also effects individual values through such a psychological path: it is in the education process that individuals develop their values and become more self-expression oriented.

Thus, both levels of analyses point to the importance of education for the forming of a more self-expression-oriented public in these societies. Education from the time of Plato, has been viewed as indispensable for democracy. For students of comparative democracy, education has been an indispensable indicator for various kinds of political behaviors, such as voting and other forms of participation. Previous chapters have linked self-expression values to political behaviors and attitudes: protest, participating in civil society, and critical citizenship. The findings presented in this chapter should lead to an optimistic note: as access to elementary, secondary, and college education keeps expanding in the East Asian societies, self-expression values will continue to rise. Citizens in these societies will continue to become active in politics, demanding more democratic and accountable political systems.

NOTES

1. I owe this multilevel design to Christian Welzel of Jacobs University, Bremen, Germany.
2. As for Korea, if we change the calculation only slightly, such as changing S_2 to be the result of 11 or 12 years of formal education, D_3 will also turn out to be smaller than D_2. Such a change should be perfectly acceptable, given that, as I said earlier, the population in Korea without a college education on average has formal years of education close to 11 or 12 years.

Part III

Self-Expression Values and Citizen Politics

Chapter 6

Self-Expression Values and Protest Potential: Challenging Authoritarianism in East Asia

The importance of protest in politics in general, and in democratization in particular, is central. Without large-scale demonstrations, rallies, sit-ins, and boycotts, many democratizations of the last 2 decades probably would not have taken place, or at least not as quickly as they did. Protests become essential channels for citizens to make their voices heard and messages received. In both democracies and nondemocracies, protest has been a political resource for citizens, a space for politics to play out, and an institution for expression. In this sense protest has been important for political changes. In democracies, political protest is a major source of pressure for improved government quality, while in nondemocracies, political protest is a major, probably *the* major, weapon of the people to press a repressive regime to loosen up and bring in liberalist reforms. Protest is, thus, an important intermediate variable for us to understand the development of democracy.

This chapter has a single task: to understand how value change can affect an individual's willingness or likelihood of resorting to political protest. One major argument of this book holds that self-expression values are important for democracy because they affect people's political behaviors, one of which is protest. Because protest is critical in bringing about political changes toward democracy, if self-expression values increase people's protest potential, then the rise of self-expression values will improve the probability of democratization.

As we saw in chapter 4, the rise of self-expression values means that people become less paternalist, prefer equal authority relationships at home and at work and between men and women, favor individual liberty vis-à-vis material and physical security, and show tolerance to differences. But what can such value changes tell us in terms of protest behaviors? At first sight, there may be no such a linkage. For example, why should one who believes in gender equality be more willing to challenge the state than one who thinks women should defer to men in social and family life? Why should one who is more tolerant toward homosexuality be more ready to take to the streets against the state?

In fact, we can argue that these values have a very strong influence on protest behaviors. As I will demonstrate, value change is more important in predicting a person's protest potential than many other factors that one might intuitively rate as important. For example, one would think that political grievance would be a stronger indicator for an individual's protest tendency, but in fact it is less so than self-expression values. In the rest of this chapter, I first give a simplified history of populist protest as the engine of political change in East Asia. Second, I examine the existing literature on protest, focusing on the studies that link value changes with protest behaviors. In the last part I carry out statistical analyses to test the causal effect of value changes on protest potential.

Protests and Democratization in East Asia

Protest takes place not just in the streets or other public spaces. Citizens can use other, less visible, forms of protest to achieve similar political goals. Petition, for example, offers a technique for advocating causes, expressing grievance, and exerting pressure on authority. Earlier seen as a form of unconventional political participation, we now accept it as a method for people to affect political outcomes. On the other hand, the politically weak can always find unique forms of protest that work best within the political space and available opportunities. Some forms of protest can appear very limited in terms of scale and visibility and, in a sense, petty. For example, scholars have identified unique forms of protest such as foot dragging by peasants working for unpleasant landlords (Scott, 1985).[1]

Weapons of the Weak

The present study looks at forms of protest that have direct interaction with state power—in other words, political techniques used by members of a civil society in their protest against state actions. We can categorize various forms of protest by their cost for the participant. That is, some forms of protest are relatively easier than others for individuals to resort to or participate in. For example, signing a petition probably involves the minimum cost for an individual to articulate interests, supply support, or express discontent outside the state apparatus. (The cost for a person to organize a petition campaign, however, is another matter.) Some forms of protest may have very high cost in terms of time, human energy, and financial as well as other resources they demand. Sitting in front of City Hall to demand government attention requires substantial amounts of these resources for the participating individual. In South Korea, during the Kwangju Movement of 1981, students protested by jumping from rooftops of buildings to kill themselves. The grievance against the repressive military regime led people to protest with their lives. In China, power abuse of local governments has resulted in peasants' setting fire to themselves. During protests against the World Trade Organization (WTO), in September 2003, a South Korean farmer killed himself by cutting into his chest with a Swiss Army knife in front of building where WTO talks were being held in Cancun, Mexico (Brooke, 2003).

Challenging Authoritarianism in East Asia

The central role that large-scale protest plays in the breakaway from authoritarian regime needs no further emphasis. Not to mention protests that led to regime changes and so-called color revolutions in Eastern and Central Europe, people power has in the past fundamentally challenged or even removed authoritarian regimes in East Asia from Myanmar to Indonesia to the Philippines to China. However, we have no better example of democratization brought about by popular protest than in South Korea, where the struggle for democracy started as early as the 1960s. By the time of its first open presidential election in 1987, the popular uprising led at least three major attempts on the life of the repressive regime.

In the 1960s, as South Korea started to modernize its economy, demand for changes in the military regime grew rapidly. Up until 1987, when the final large-scale demonstration directly resulted in the abolition of the military regime and the first free and open presidential election, three major uprisings had taken place in Korea's long struggle for democracy: the 1960 uprising, the 1980 Kwanju Massacre, and the 1987 People's March. Violent demonstrations continued all through these periods. In the early and mid-1980s, some 70 incidents of self-immolation took place as protest against the government for citizen's basic democratic rights, as well as those who jumped to their deaths from buildings (Kim, 1987, cited in Oh, 1999). Finally, in 1987, the demand for democracy exploded into marches in Seoul and almost all important urban centers in the country, with the number of participants increasing each day. On June 26, it culminated in the Great Peace March of the People. On June 29, the regime surrendered and agreed to hold the country's first free presidential election.

If South Korea presents the most enduring struggle of the weak challenging the repressive state, it is certainly not the only one. In fact, all the successful transitions to democracy in East Asia were associated with large-scale civil disobedience in the form of protests and demonstrations. In 1986, popular protest ended the dictatorship of Marcos in the Philippines and returned the country to an electoral democracy. In late 1989, the same year which saw the Tiananmen student movement repressed in China, students and intellectuals protested in Ulan Bator demanding democracy and respect for human rights. In the new year, the government legalized opposition parties and held open elections (Rossabi, 1992). Some believe Beijing's forceful repression of student demonstrations set a negative example for Mongolian authorities who dropped force as an option in dealing with the protesters (Rossabi, 1992). In the year following the military takeover of power in Thailand in 1991, large-scale citizen protests ended military rule and set the country on a course of consolidating democracy. In Indonesia in 1998, months of antigovernment protests resulted directly in Shuharto's resignation and the first free parliament election in the country's history since Independence. In Taiwan, the opposition had engaged in protests since the 1960s, and in March 1990, held a large-scale student demonstration in Taipei demanding further political reform. At its peak, more than 5,000 participated in the sit-in (Ho, 2003; Wright, 2001). In 1992 Taiwan held the first direct election for its national legislation and in 1996 the first direct presidential election, completing the transition to democracy. The following table sums up these developments between popular protests and democratization in East Asia in the late 20th century (Table 6.1).

This table reveals the relationship between civil society pressure and political change. For countries where authoritarianism took root, civil uprising is always important in bringing democratization to the top of the national agenda. At such a point, actions of the elite become important: to either respond to people's demands, or to repress them. Other factors become

Table 6.1. Popular protests and democratization in East Asia.

Countries	*Major Uprisings/Protests*	*Year of Democratization*
South Korea	1980, 1981, 1987	1987
Taiwan	1990	1986–1992
Philippines	1986	1986
Mongolia	1989–1990	1990
Thailand	1992	1992
Indonesia	1998	1998–2000

Source. Author.

important only then, such as foreign intervention or the stance of religious leaders (see Huntington, 1991). In the case of South Korea, for example, the fact the U.S. urged the government not to use force in the 1987 demonstration proved critical—but critical only when there was already a large-scale demonstration and the regime was in peril. Public pressure, mostly expressed in protests and demonstration, set the structural conditions under which elite political games unfold.

Values, Protest, and Politics

Why do people protest? Politically, public discontent or distrust of government can lead to protest. Socially, changing social structure may create new conditions conducive to protest. The rise of feminism or environmentalism can also drive social protests. Sociological studies of protests tend to focus on the "opportunity structure" of social actors and the resources the actors command for organization and mobilization (Tarrow, 1998). Because protests depend on many factors, grievance does not always translate into public protest, for example when the actors failed to identify a common object toward which to direct their grievance (Javeline, 2003). With a similar amount of resources, one protest cascaded while the other did not because the opportunity structures perceived by the two groups of protesters differed (Wright, 2001).

This chapter focuses on the argument that, as a society acquires stronger self-expression values, its citizens will likely become more prepared to resort to protest as a way of political expression. In classical studies of social and political changes, socioeconomic modernization changes politics because first it changes political actors—individual human beings (Almond & Verba, 1963; Lipset, 1960). Modernization generally results in increased demand for political participation by the masses (Deutsch, 1961; Huntington & Nelson, 1976). In more recent scholarship, others find that people with higher socioeconomic status or educational levels will more likely participate in protests (Norris, 1999a).

But we cannot simply say as people become more well-off, they will likely cause trouble for the government. Affluence itself does not lead to a higher likelihood of protest behaviors. In fact, it is generally argued that the better-off in a society will more likely lean toward protecting the status quo, instead of challenging the system. Rather, the value changes within an individual caused by a rising level of affluence make the difference. Inglehart's postmaterialism concept offers an explanation of why socioeconomic development translates into cognitive or psychological changes of citizens (Barnes & Kaase, 1979; Inglehart, 1977). People of stronger postmaterialist orientation will more likely resort to unconventional political participation, such as demonstrations.

Inglehart's explanation holds that postmaterialists have less concern with immediate issues related to daily existence, such as food and shelter. Instead, they have the resources (time and energy), the skills (cognitive mobilization), and the propensity to concern themselves with issues of broader and longer-term significance, such as government efficiency and environmental quality. As a result, they become more likely to join protests demanding democracy and policy changes (Inglehart, 1990).

Nevertheless, the shift in people's priorities from economic and physical security to freedom of expression and environmental protection alone still does not explain the rise in protests. We must look at the cognitive processes of individuals to understand why some people may consider certain actions. Each individual has an internal cognitive structure, through which we process information. People with different cognitive structures will likely come to different conclusions in response to similar information. One's values largely define one's cognitive structure, and people with different values will likely reach different conclusions when receiving the same set of information, given their different cognitive structures. One concludes that some action of the state is unacceptable because there is a discrepancy between one's ideal and the message one receives. Under such circumstance, protest becomes a possible behavioral response.

Self-expression values comprise a set of values: valuing liberty and empowerment through participatory rights, tolerance of differences, rejecting paternalism and patriarchy, pursuit of leisure, and supporting gender equality. Individuals with such values or beliefs have greater sensitivity to unfair institutions or unjust state actions. In other words, their information processing will more likely result in discrepancies between the political reality (especially under a repressive regime) and their cognitive structures. Because values structure one's information processing, values determine the cognitive outcomes: the conclusions regarding acceptability of a political situation. With negative conclusions, protest becomes a viable behavioral choice.

Studies have found some values increase an individual's protest potential. If one develops values that stress self- actualization, he or she will more likely challenge the status quo (Flanagan & Lee, 2000). Therefore, one's values shape the cognitive process that result in an inclination toward protest options. Inglehart and colleagues' analyses focus on the relationship between self-expression values and the level of democracy of a certain society. They argue that self-expression values stress personal empowerment, liberty, and equality—a set of emancipative values. Such people are more sensitive to injustices in the status quo and more ready to formulate alternatives and express demand for change (Welzel, Inglehart & Klingemann, 2003). In other words, they have higher protest potential. The pursuit of empowerment can be easily translated into the desire for political participation. When the motive to participate is high, and the existing political institutions do not provide accessible and effective channels, cognitive discrepancy will result. In turn, protest can become a response.

That value change leads people to protest is indeed another way to say that, with the rise of self-expression values, people will more likely openly demand political changes. These changes can be small ones, such as changes in a local policy. They can be intermediate, such as changes in political ideas or party platforms. They can be big ones: changes of political leaders and ruling parties. They can also be fundamental changes of political institutions: from a one-party dominant system to a competitive multiparty democracy. Given this understanding, we believe the rise of self-expression values means the increasing probability of political liberalization in an authoritarian regime, and the increased quality of democracy in an already democratized society.

Self-Expression Values and Protest Potential

Measuring Protest Potential

In the current study, we measure protest potential by asking whether people have recently done or might consider using several forms of unconventional participation methods. Five forms of protest are considered: (1) signing a petition, (2) joining a boycott, (3) attending a demonstration, (4) joining a strike, and (5) occupying buildings. For each of these forms of protest, those who reported that they have recently (in the past 5 years or so) done so are coded as "1," those who reported that they might do it are coded as "2," and those who reported that they would never, under any conditions, do it, are coded as "3." Table 6.2 shows the percentage of responses to these questions. Note that the five societies in which these questions were asked are grouped as democracies (Japan, South Korea, and Taiwan) and nondemocracies (Singapore and Vietnam).

Protest potential has two characteristics: first, there are high correlations among a person's willingness to use different forms of protest; a person more willing to sign a petition, for example, will also more likely resort to other forms of protest, such as attending a demonstration. Second, some forms of protest are

Table 6.2. Protest behaviors in East Asia (percentage of people who either have recently done or might do the following in the future).

	Nondemocracy	*Democracy*
	Percentage (Valid N)	*Percentage (Valid N)*
Signing petition	49.9% 2,900	76.8% 4,103
Boycott	17.5% 2,859	58.3% 3,646
Demonstration	33.0% 2,897	51.0% 3,752
Strike	10.8% 1,382	32.9% 3,691
Occupying building	23.4% 1,269	7.0% 2,601

more difficult for individuals to participate in than the others. For example, the percentage of people who have or might use petition is much larger than that of occupying a building.

To construct a single measurement of protest potential, I exclude strikes and occupation of buildings, as these two did not appear in the Singapore survey. Then for each of the three forms of protest behaviors, those who responded either "have done" or "might do" are coded as "1," while those reported "would never do" are coded as "0." We now have three dichotomous variables, and we can see that about one third would never use any protest actions, while something between a quarter and one third who would use all three kinds of protest.

Some forms of protest appear more costly for individuals than others. For example, for those individuals willing to

Table 6.3. Proportions of citizens who would use protest options.

	Frequency	*Valid Percent*
Will NEVER use ANY form of protest	2,022	32.8%
Will use ONE (1) form of protest	1,204	19.6%
Will use TWO (2) forms of protest	1,211	19.7%
Will use THREE (3) forms of protest	1,718	27.9%
Total	6,155[a]	100.0%

Source. WVS, 1999–2001, South Korea, Japan, Singapore, Vietnam; WVS, 1995, Taiwan; where South Korea, Japan, and Taiwan are categorized as democracies, and Singapore and Vietnam are nondemocracies.
[a]The cases with missing values are exaggerated by the fact that this is a scale generated by adding three variables together. Thus, even if only one variable has a missing value, the new scale is coded as missing.

sign a petition, only a little more than half (58%) will attend a demonstration, and only about 70% are willing to join a boycott. On the other hand, among those willing to attend a demonstration, almost all—94%—will sign a petition. The correlation between boycott and petition is similar; of those willing to join a boycott, 97% would sign a petition. Thus, the cost for attending a demonstration is about twice as high as that of signing a petition, and that of signing a petition is about 70% of that of joining a boycott. Based on this differentiation, to calculate a composite index of protest potential, I give the weight of 1 to petition, 1.5 to boycott, and 2 to demonstration, adding them together to have a variable with the range of 0–4.5.

Independent Variables

We intend to determine whether self-expression values has a significant effect on an individual's protest potential, with self-expression values as the major independent variable. Other independent variables include political discontent, political trust, life satisfaction, and support of democracy. I also include a person's interest in politics (e.g., following political news) as a major controlling variable, and several important control variables, such as educational backgrounds. First, let me explain these variables in some detail.

Political Discontent

Political discontent is important because it is natural to hypothesize that people who are dissatisfied with current political development are more likely to protest. Here we need to pay attention to two questions: (1) Does political discontent have a significant effect on protest potential? and (2) how big is its effect compared to that of self-expression values. In other words, which is more important or consequential: deep-rooted values or (temporary) assessment of a current political development?

Our survey data allow us to measure political discontent using several questions, concerning the overall development of democracy, the status of human rights, the performance of the incumbent government, and the fairness of the system. Here are the questions:

1. Overall Satisfaction: *On the whole, are you very satisfied, rather satisfied, not very satisfied, or not at all satisfied with the way democracy is developing in our country? (1–4 ordinal scale)*
2. Human Rights: *How much respect is there for individual human rights nowadays (in our country)? Do you feel*

there is a lot of respect, some respect, not much respect, or no respect at all? (1–4 ordinal scale)

3. Incumbent Satisfaction: *How satisfied are you with the way people now in national office are handling the country's affairs? Would you say you are very satisfied, fairly satisfied, fairly dissatisfied, or very dissatisfied? (1–4 ordinal scale)*
4. Fairness of the System: *Generally speaking, would you say that this country is run by a few big interests looking out for themselves, or that it is run for the benefit of all the people? (1–2 ordinal scale)*

These four questions are included in a factor analysis to generate a score of political discontent for each country.

Trust in Formal Institutions: Political Distrust

One might hypothesize that when people have low trust in formal political institutions, they will more likely employ options of protest. In fact, street politics—called protests by some and extraparliamentary politics by others—takes place outside the formal institutions of political participation and interest aggregation. In this study, each respondent is asked about his or her confidence in various political institutions, such as parliament, the national government, the civil service, and the police. A political trust score is calculated using factor analysis.

Life Satisfaction

The effect of life satisfaction on protest may be difficult to predict. On the one hand, those who are satisfied will protest less, while those who perceive adversity and privation may want to express discontent. On the other hand, people who are satisfied with life as a whole are more likely to be postmaterialists, and as the now well-known postmaterialism argument points out, these individuals tend to be more politically active. Those who join new social movements (environmentalism, women's rights and antiwar movements in Western Europe and North America) normally come from relatively well-off backgrounds.

To test the effect of life satisfaction on protest, I calculate a score of life satisfaction from three variables: one's satisfaction with the overall financial situation in her household (1–10 ordinal scale), one's satisfaction with her life as a whole (1–10 ordinal scale), and one's happiness level in general (1–4 ordinal scale).

Support for Democracy

Support for democracy, as discussed in chapter 2, gauges a person's overt attitude toward democracy (Chu, Diamond & Shin, 2001; Dalton & Ong, 2003; Dalton & Shin, 2003). I use the formula of "supporting democracy minus supporting nondemocratic governance" to measure an individual's overt support of democracy (Klingemann, 1999). The indicator is calculated as (A + B) – (C + D) below (all are of 1–4 ordinal scale):

A. *Having a democratic political system is: very good, fairly good, bad, or very bad;*
B. *Democracy may have problems, but it's better than any other form of government: agree strongly, agree, disagree, or strongly disagree;*

C. *Having a strong leader who does not have to bother with parliament and elections is very good, fairly good, bad, or very bad;*
D. *Having experts, not government, make decisions according to what they think is best for the country is very good, fairly good, bad, or very bad.*

Political Interest

Political interest will probably have a strong effect on protest potential. From very early, we have known socioeconomic development is accompanied by cognitive mobilization of individuals, of which improved interest in politics is one major component (Inglehart, 1977, 1990). I include political interest as a major controlling variable. It is a factor score of the four questions asked in the survey:

How important is politics in your life (from 4: very important to 1: not at all important)?

When you get together with your friends, would you say you discuss political matters frequently, occasionally, or never (coded 3, 2, 1, respectively)?

How interested would you say you are in politics (from 4: very interested to 1: not at all interested)?

How often do you follow politics in the news on television or on the radio or in the daily papers? (from 5: every day to 1: never)

Social and Demographic Variables

I also include social and demographic variables, such as gender, age groups, marital status, and educational backgrounds. Professional background is also included because it is generally believed that white collar and professionals are more politically engaged than, say, manual laborers and agricultural workers (Norris, 2002).

Multivariate Analysis

In the first place, it is probably useful to take a general look at how each independent variable might affect the dependent variable. The following table shows the proportion of respondents that would use various kinds of protest methods, looking at the impact of the various independent variables.

The table barely needs explanation. The major independent variables, self-expression values, political interest, political discontent, and political distrust, all have a clear effect on protest potential. Basically, high values of all these four independent variables point to higher protest potential. Also, people with a high level of support for democracy show a higher level of protest potential. As I suggested above, the effect of life satisfaction is not that clear. People with high levels of life satisfaction basically do not seem to have higher level of protest potential. The proportion of people willing to sign a petition is significantly higher than that of attending a demonstration or joining a boycott, supporting the claim that the costs of different forms protest are different, at least as perceived by the individual.

Assuming that the relationship between protest potential and the various independent variables may not be the same in different societies, I conduct one regression analysis for each society. The results of the analyses are presented in Table 6.5.

A long process of statistical operations produced Table 6.5. In the process I experimented with various ways to find a regression model that captures the largest portion of the story in the most concise and understandable form. The decision to include the current independent variables in the model, and to include them in the current form, came after such a long process. That

Table 6.4. Protest potential and independent variables (percentage of people who either have recently done or might do the following in the future).

	Self-Expression Values		*Political Interest*		*Political Discontent*		*Political Distrust*		*Life Satisfaction*		*Support of Democracy*	
	Low	*High*	*Low*	*High*	*Low*	*High*	*Low*	*High*	*Low*	*High*	*Low*	*High*
	% (*Valid N*)	% (*Valid N*)	% (*Valid N*)	% (*Valid N*)	% (*Valid N*)	% (*Valid N*)	% (*Valid N*)	% (*Valid N*)	% (*Valid N*)	% (*Valid N*)	% (*Valid N*)	% (*Valid N*)
Petition	58.5%[a]	73.3%[b]	58.7%	71.4%	62.2%	72.1%	69.1%	76.7%	68.7%	68.4%	61.1%	76.5%
	3,289	2,736	3,127	3,578	3,968	2,275	2,175	2,351	2,381	3,017	1,282	4,917
Boycott	32.5%	48.2%	34.1%	45.5%	35.6%	48.9%	40.3%	57.0%	46.3%	45.8%	30.9%	59.5%
	3,075	2,552	2,920	3,323	3,720	2,132	1,987	2,113	2,166	2,818	1,242	4,654
Demonstration	35.8%	51.8%	34.9%	51.3%	39.9%	51.8%	47.6%	52.6%	44.1%	43.7%	43.2%	49.6%
	3,157	2,607	2,998	3,389	3,784	2,155	2,047	2,169	2,231	2,858	1,248	4,695

Source. WVS, 1999–2001, South Korea, Japan, Vietnam, and Singapore; WVS, 1995, Taiwan.

[a,b]The percentages of these two columns in general should *not* add up to 100%. These figures represent the percentage of people among those with low or high self-expression values, respectively, who have or might sign a petition. Thus, 3,289 respondents had self-expression values lower than zero, and among them, 58.5% have done or would sign a petition; 2,736 respondents had self- expression values higher than zero, and among them 73.3% have done or would sign a petition. The above is true for the other columns and rows.

Table 6.5. Protest potential in five East Asian societies.

Dependent Variable: Protest Potential: Have you done, might do, or will never do these: signing a petition, joining a boycott, attending a demonstration?

	Beta (SE)				
	Japan	*Korea*	*Taiwan*	*Vietnam*	*Singapore*
Self-Expression Values	.38 (.08)***	.30 (.07)***	.14 (.01)	.20 (.05)***	.22 (.04)***
Political Distrust	.24 (.08)**	.04 (.07)	.06 (.01)	–.03 (.06)	(NA)
Political Discontent	–.03 (.08)	.14 (.07)*	–.01 (.01)	.02 (.06)	.22 (.04)***
Life Satisfaction	.06 (.07)	.06 (.06)	–.02 (.01)	.01 (.05)	–.08 (.04)*
Political Interest	.30 (.08)***	.24 (.04)***	.54 (.09)***	.16 (.06)*	.23 (.04)***
Support of Democracy	.03 (.04)	.00 (.04)	–.02 (.07)	.11 (.05)*	–.03 (.04)
Social and Demographic					
Male (0–1)	.35 (.15)*	.25 (.13)*	.09 (.21)	–.03 (.11)	.02 (.09)
Age groups (1–6)	.10 (.06)*	–.24 (.07)***	–.21 (.08)**	–.05 (.04)	–.09 (.04)*
Single (0–1)	–.23 (.17)	–.43 (.17)*	.13 (.25)	.37 (.14)*	.37 (.10)***
Education Level (1–6)	.01 (.08)	.23 (.10)*	.07 (.09)	.07 (.06)	.08 (.04)*
Professional Background					
Managerial/Business Owners	.53 (.28)*	.27 (.27)	.07 (.69)	.05 (.20)	–.19 (.20)
Professional (Lawyer, etc.)	.44 (.12)	.03 (.30)	.85 (.74)	–.38 (.18)*	.07 (.16)
Other White Collar	.47 (.26)*	.48 (.25)*	.37 (.71)	–.08 (.15)	–.35 (.17)*
Skilled Manual Labor	.25 (.31)	.23 (.31)	.17 (.69)	–.05 (.15)	–.23 (.12)*
Unskilled Manual Labor and Agricultural Worker	–.04 (.28)	.41 (.33)	.52 (.67)	Excluded	–.45 (.13)**
R-Square	.139	.166	.201	.051	.182

*α < 0.1; **α < 0.01; ***<0.001

is to say, these are methodologically rigorous results, and we can discuss their theoretical implications.

Self-Expression Values and Other Attitudinal Variables

One irrefutable finding is the strong effect of self-expression values on protest potential. With the exception of Taiwan, it has a statistically very significant and large effect (ranging from 0.219 for Singapore to 0.377 for Japan). Among these countries, the size of the effect of self-expression values is the largest, except for Singapore, where its effect is only slightly smaller than political interest. The effects of other independent variables, such as political discontent and political distrust are relatively smaller. Even in Taiwan, although the effect of self-expression values is not statistically significant (at 0.1 level), in terms of size, it is still larger than those variables (with the exception of political interest). After controlling self-expression values, political distrust and discontent with current political development have basically no significant effect on the individual's willingness to protest. Nor do support for democracy or life satisfaction. Except for an individual's interest in politics, self-expression values is the only variable that can account for an individual's willingness to join protest actions.

Other Variables

As for socioeconomic variables, the results show that education has a big effect in Korea and not in any other society. (In Singapore the effect is significant, but the size is small.) This is probably because the effect of education is already accounted for by self-expression values and other psychological and cognitive propensities, such as an individual's political interest. People with higher levels of education are also high in self-expression values and have stronger interest in politics. In terms of age, younger people seem to be more ready to use protest options. We need not explain this given the amount of scholarship arguing cultural shift through generational replacement in modernizing societies (Inglehart, 1988). But for the case of Japan, younger people are indeed less likely to use protest than the older ones. Although in most of the postindustrial societies in Europe and North America, young people tend to participate actively in protests such as anti-war and environmental movements, in Japan one sees a largely inactive and indifferent youth. Indeed, my data does show political interest among young people in Japan is low.

The shift toward a prodemocracy mass culture comes along with the rise of postindustrial society. In line with this, we would expect to find people in the service sector (white collar and knowledge professions) and those of a managerial background having higher political activism. But the findings here present a more complex picture. It seems that in democracies (Japan, Korea, and Taiwan), white collar workers and people in managerial and professional careers show a higher level of protest potential than the society as a whole, although some of these effects are not significant statistically. On the contrary, in nondemocracies, these people show a lower level of protest potential. Institutional factors may play a role here. For example, comparing Japan, Korea, and Taiwan, and also perhaps Singapore and Vietnam, the government has a better institutional framework to co-opt social and professional elites. This is highly plausible. Some have argued that dependence upon the state would prevent business and social elites from challenging the state (Bellin, 2000). Or, maybe in these two societies, sufficiently developed formal channels of participation satisfy the aggregating interests of the social and professional elites. Hence these elites find it natural to work with the establishment. Indeed, both Singapore and Vietnam have higher levels of political trust or political content than do the democracies, thus appearing to support these two possible explanations.

Conclusion

Analyses in this chapter find self-expression values a very strong factor when it comes to explaining political activism. Let us recall what the term *self-expression values* means: this concept refers to a syndrome of value changes that takes place in modernizing societies. Such a syndrome comprises several important dimensions of human value with regard to personal and social life (Tables 4.1 and 4.2). Although holding these values may not translate into an individual's overt demand for democratic government, in daily life, regarding each issue that affects them personally, such an individual will likely make more democratic choices. Such individuals have a stronger sense of justice and fairness and respect for individual rights and freedom, hence they will likely demand changes to better protect these values. Holding other things equal, a rise in self-expression values among the populace translates into a higher likelihood of protests. Other factors, such as a high level of political distrust, political discontent, or life dissatisfaction are less essential. Nor does a high level of public support for democracy matter much.

For the analysis of real political developments, we can probably construct such a picture: high level of self-expression values means a high readiness for the public to engage in protest actions. High levels of political discontent, political distrust, and grievance will trigger real protest actions. Hence, socio-economic developments, by generating a high-level of self-expression values, provide a structural factor for protests to take place, while the contingent factors of distrust in government, political discontent, and grievance usher in actions. Whether potential translates into action depends largely on these as well as other contingent factors, such as the existence, strength, and strategies of mobilization. Thus, the rise of self-expression contributes to political changes.

Postscript: Protest in Early 21st-Century China

Although this chapter's analysis does not include China, I will devote an extra section to dwell on this issue. Starting from the late 1990s, mass protests took central stage in Chinese politics. China's official figures put the number of "collective incidents" at 87,000 for 2005, up from 74,000 in 2004, and almost nine times that of 1993. And this does not include either peaceful (such as petitions, letters, and office visits) or individual protests. How do we understand this in light of the findings of this chapter?

Most importantly, one should note that protests in China largely fall into two categories. The first includes protests against government acts that immediately violate citizen interests, the most notable being the government's appropriation of land. Others involve illicit use of public funds or properties. For example, in 2005, in Shanwei, Guangdong Province, a peasant protest escalated into confrontation with armed police. According to Western media, as many as 20 peasants were killed.

Protesters of this first category come from so-called disadvantaged groups, such as land-deprived peasants, unpaid migrant workers, and resettled city residents. They protest because their livelihood or properties are infringed upon or threatened. Some protests, such as peasant protests against local taxation documented by scholars like Yu Jianrong, are well organized (Yu, 2003), and they can use violent and radical means. In many cases, more than a thousand protesters have stormed a town hall. In other cases, protesters set fire to government cars and vans. In Ya'an, Sichuan Province, in November 2004, protesters stormed the city government hall and held the provincial party secretary Zhang Xuezhong, who was on a working tour, besieged in the building for more than a day. More scattered protests have seen individuals setting fires to themselves (at a public square or in front of a city government hall and in several cases at Tiananmen Square in Beijing), throwing themselves from atop a building, or taking innocent people hostage (most of the time children) as a way of demanding government concessions.

Localized and largely containable by the government, such protests can be called *pocket unrest.* They comprise the overwhelming majority of the collective incidents in China. As many have rightly pointed out, correct solutions lie in correcting government policies and taking seriously the interests of the disadvantaged. The central government seems serious about this under its "harmonious society" banner. But whether it can make things work at the local government level is a different matter entirely. Research shows that protesters still trust the central government's commitment to the welfare of the common folk, and they direct grievances mostly toward local abusers. But research also shows that once protests fail to extract remedies from the government, trust in the central government decreases. It follows that citizens may challenge the legitimacy of the central government as such disillusions accumulate.

The second kind of protest transcends age, gender, social group, and locality. These protests signal the increasing readiness of Chinese citizens to publicly express their demands. Such is an outcome of the rising self-expression values among the Chinese public. Demands put forward by protesters may not stem directly from government abuses: protesters may have participated not because their property was confiscated or their rights threatened, but because of issues that have broader implications. The anti-Japanese demonstrations seen in several major cities in spring 2005 offer one example. A related incident occurred when more than one million citizens endorsed a petition (mostly on-line) in protest against the Ministry of Railways for wanting to contract the Beijing–Shanghai high-speed rail to Japanese companies. In other cases, petitioners protested against the government's discriminatory policies: one policy involved discrimination against hepatitis B virus carriers; another involved discrimination against migrant workers. Petitions by environmentalists also resulted in the central government's re-examining a planned hydropower station in Yunnan Province.

Unlike pocket unrest, this second kind of protest has a social movement nature. Today's social movements around the globe generally mobilize around postmodern issues, such as environmentalism, gay rights, women's rights, and minority rights (also antiwar and antiglobalization). While peasant unrest can be extremely radical and violent, social movement protests are mostly peaceful and rational. They also involve a more educated population and mobilize participants from all walks of life. The protesters also have better knowledge, resources, and mobilization technologies, such as Internet bulletin boards and cell phone messages. In this sense, they are indeed much more difficult for the regime to manage.

If the solution to pocket unrest is what the Party hailed as to build a "harmonious society," then it has probably no solution to social movement protests. The critical implication of this chapter is that, due to the rising self-expression values, citizens in a modernizing society are bound to become more assertive in voicing their demands. As China gets richer, its disadvantaged groups may fare better, but protests by environmentalists and human and civil rights supporters will rise. In the long run, therefore, if the regime continues to deliver economic development, pocket unrests may decrease, but social movement protests will, ironically, increase. The solution, then, is not suppression, but recognition of people's right to expression. The government must legalize protests while at the same time finding the right ways to manage them. This probably points the way to ultimate harmony: assume public expression as a legitimate part of democratic life.

NOTE

1. See also Chen, Calvin. "Working Around the Rules: Chinese Workers and Their Informal Strategies of Survival." *Paper presented at the annual meeting of the American Political Science Association, Philadelphia, PA, 2003-08-27.*

Chapter 7

Self-Expression Values and the Infrastructure of Democracy

Civil society has become a central subject for scholars of democracy, and scholars of both democratization and scholars of advanced democracies acknowledge its significance. Scholars of democratization argue that civil society is instrumental in both democratic transition and democratic consolidation (Gill, 2000; Grugel, 2002; Linz & Stepan, 1996; Pridham, 2000), while the latter argue that a strong civil society directly leads to a high quality of democratic governance (Couto & Guthrie, 1999). No recent work in this area has influenced the field more than that of Putnam (1993, 2000). For him, dense associational networks and the high social trust resulting from these networks—namely, *social capital*—provide the solid social foundation that "makes democracy work." On the other hand, the troublesomely low participation of American citizens in politics (such as voting), goes hand-in-glove with civil society breakdown, such as the disappearance of bowling leagues in the United States.

This civil society or social capital argument seems to have struck a chord, given the many international development programs that currently aim at promoting democracy and good governance through civil society. Nonetheless, debate continues concerning which kinds of civic groups positively affect democracy, which do not, as well as how civil society can play a role in democratization. Scholars continue to debate that social capital such as trust will grow out of voluntary associations; that social trust can lead to political trust, which in turn promotes democratic governance; and that a high level of social trust correlates to a high quality of democracy (Newton, 2001). Some attempt to redefine the concept of civil society, arguing that citizens' participation patterns have shifted toward more radical kinds of involvement, such as protests (Welzel, Inglehart, & Deutsch, 2005). More empirical research, however, continue to emerge arguing for the important supporting role civil society plays in the consolidation and functioning of democracy (Boussard, 2003; Couto & Guthrie, 1999; Varshney, 2002).

I will first review the literature on civil society and social capital, focusing on the role of civil society in democratization and democratic consolidation. Then, I present my empirical tests to find out the relationship between self-expression values and engagement in civil society. The empirical section of this chapter examines whether individual values can affect citizen's engagement in civil society, as measured by joining and volunteering for social groups. If higher self-expression values translate into more active engagement in civil society, then rising self-expression values will result in denser associational networks, which in turn mean a more active civil society and higher social capital. It follows that rising self-expression values mean better social foundations for democracy: it will mean better preparedness for democratization or a higher social capital that will help increase the quality of an already democratic government.

Civil Society and Democracy

It seems any discussion of civil society and social capital must start from Putnam's *Making Democracy Work* (1993). But indeed this only represents one of two lines of intellectual discourse and empirical research. The discourse of social capital largely concerns itself with good governance and community building, while that of civil society focuses more on democratization: transition as well as consolidation. Furthermore, simply talking about civic networks as social capital is not enough. One has to ask: what kind of civic networks for which kinds of civic groups can increase domestic conflicts, thus deteriorating democratic life? (Varshney, 2002) In the limited space below, I will focus on civil society's role in democratization.

A Tale of Two Discourses

Studies of civil society and social capital both focus on associational networks. These networks, although existing at the grassroots level, have important political consequences. But concepts and the discourses descended from them have separate intellectual origins. In political science, the concept of social capital emerged from a study of the quality of democracy (Putnam,

1993), while that of civil society emerged from contentious citizen politics in former Communist countries eventually resulting in the fall of those regimes (Geremek, 1996). The discourse of social capital continues to focus on how dense citizen networks can be instrumental in facilitating political participation, trust in government, and closer ties between state and citizens (e.g., Putnam, 2000). On the other hand, the discourse of civil society has more and more focused on the contentious sphere of citizen politics. In advanced democracies, this means especially civil society's mobilizing capacity in various new social movements (e.g., Norris, 2002). In developing countries, this normally means civil society's role in challenging the authoritarian government and negotiating a more democratic state–society relationship (Heryanto & Mandal, 2003). Civil society, in this regard, includes various movements: labor movements, women's movements, human rights movements, indigenous movements, and community movements (Grugel, 2002).

So how does civil society play a role in democratization? It first started with the dissident movements in Communist Europe in the late 1970s. Czech Charter 77 defined a collective movement of intellectuals, journalists, and artists who wanted to voice their dissent against a repressive Communist regime (Havel, 1985). The Solidarity Labor Union of Poland had the same purpose, and by the end of the 1980s it had succeeded in bringing down a regime (Geremek, 1996). Civil society, at least at that time, meant organized disobedience. Solidarity struggled until the fall of Communism, 1989–1991, when it came to the attention of scholars and policy makers in the West. Also at this time, a thesis of social capital came out in Italy, considered an advanced democracy. This followed Putnam's important book, *Making*

Democracy Work, based on his long study (which, coincidentally, also dated back to the late 1970s). In this sense one can say, in the early 1990s, two discourses that had originated and developed separately met each other. In the future they would communicate and sometimes even fuse into one, as manifested by the various international development programs of the 1990s.

Civil Society and Democratization

In any case, after the 1989 political earthquake, the post-Communist world emerged with different levels of success. Amid the political, social, and economic difficulties common in post-transition countries, if there is a clear winner, it is the idea of civil society. Suddenly we attribute every major success of democracy to civil society, moving even far beyond the creation of the term: the labor movement was instrumental through the demise of Franco's dictatorship in Spain (1939–1976), prohuman rights group such as Citizens Dignity or Memorial asserted citizens' rights against the Soviet state in the late 1980s, and indigenous movements enabled peasants to contest the terms and practices of citizenship in various Latin American countries (see a discussion in Grugel, 2002).

Indeed, such an intellectual euphoria is largely overdue. While it is clear, as in the cases of South Korea, Thailand, the Philippines, Poland, and others, large scale demonstrations in the name of the People did directly lead to the success of democracy, we can hardly attribute all these success to civil society—at least not if we define civil society as voluntary civic, social, professional, or leisure groups. In the cases listed above (Franco's Spain, Gorbachev's Soviet Union, and cases in Latin America), with state relaxation of repression, citizen groups took newly emerging political opportunities and rose to assert citizens' rights against the state. Of course, such actions on the part of these groups probably consolidated the gain in democratic relaxation, and they increased the pressure on the government to continue such relaxations. Furthermore, we must recognize the important mobilizing effect of these groups during large-scale demonstrations. Nonetheless, it is far from certain that citizen groups are so powerful as to directly lead to regime breakdown.

That is to say, we still need a clear distinction between civil society and opposition. It is true that civil groups have the potential to develop into opposition movements, sometimes even very strong oppositions, as the histories of Charter 77 and Solidarity have shown. But such a development necessarily transfigures the question—by the time these groups engage directly in competing for political power, they stop being part of the civil society. Indeed, Diamond (1996) has clearly included in the definition of civil society a nonpolitical criterion. His encyclopedic list of civil society includes only groups that are economic, cultural, informational and educational, interested based, developmental, issue oriented, and, not surprisingly, civic. Civic groups, however, participate in politics in a nonpolitical (or, rather, nonpartisan) manner, such as in human rights' monitoring, voter education, and anticorruption efforts.

Civil Society as Infrastructure of Democracy

Thus, on the system level, civil society contributes to democratization in two visible ways. First, strong opposition movements may grow out of civil activities. In extreme cases, this can directly lead to democratic transition. Second, civil groups can take newly emerging political opportunities as the authoritarian regime loses the will or the capacity to sustain its firm grip on political power. This way, civil society can serve important functions: it can check state power, assert citizens' rights, consolidate public space as it becomes newly available, and exert pressure on the state to continue relaxing its grip on power. In this way, we can appropriately view civil society as negotiating with, instead of opposing, the state. As one author argues, civil society does not aim to transform the state but to democratize society (Atienza, 1994).

Does this conceptual clarification degrade the importance of the civil society? This asks the wrong question. This clarification only means that the development of an opposition movement has its own logic and should be the focus of a different inquiry. With this clarification, we achieve conceptual coherence on the basis of which we can do empirical analyses—solving methodological issues on the basis of conceptual clarity. This will set up the second part of this chapter, where we analyze the impact of self-expression values on civil society.

On the other hand, by stripping away what does not belong to our concept, it allows us to see where the true importance of civil society lies: its importance lies more in the facilitation, rather than the initiation, of democratic transition. For this purpose, Diamond (1996) provides a list of the functions of civil society. Civil society as networks of active citizens, he argues, does have important functions in democratization. These functions mostly serve the consolidation process:

1. limiting state power and subject governments to public scrutiny, that is, to monitor democratic states and democratize authoritarian states;

2. supplementing the role of political parties in stimulating political participation, increasing their democratic awareness and skills;
3. offering a space for the development of democratic values such as tolerance, moderation, and a willingness to compromise;
4. creating channels other than political parties for the articulation, aggregation, and representation of interests, generating opportunities for participation in various levels of governance;
5. cutting across interests and mitigating the principal polarities of political conflict;
6. recruiting and training new political leaders, providing nonpartisan election monitoring, and monitoring judicial and legal reform in new democracies, a task called democracy-building;
7. disseminating information and, if necessary, contradicting official information;
8. facilitating and supporting economic reform; and
9. as a result of all the above, strengthening the state.

Thus, in the end, civil society does not overtly oppose the state, something noted as a radical perspective of civil society (Grugel, 2002). Rather, Diamond argues that "by enhancing the accountability, responsiveness, inclusiveness, effectiveness, and hence the legitimacy of the political system, a vigorous civil society gives citizens respect for the state and positive engagement with it" (Diamond, 1996, p. 234). Here it looks like we have looped the loop: that is, the gap between the concept of civil society and the concept of social capital is now undetectable. Civil society, when defined as NGOs and voluntary networks, can most appropriately be conceptualized as infrastructure of democracy. Looked at in this way, the term *social capital* becomes intelligible, and the discourse of civil society is indeed a part of the on-going debate of citizen politics (Almond & Verba, 1963; Inglehart, 1990; Putnam, 2000).

Self-Expression Values and Civil Society

After clarifying the conceptual issues, we can test whether self-expression values lead to a more active civil society. Conceptually, such an empirical investigation appears straightforward. We need to find out whether individuals with higher self-expression values will more likely participate in civil society. With the understanding that a smooth consolidation of democracy requires an active civil society, if self-expression values positively relate to engagement in civil society, then rising self-expression values means brighter prospects for democracy.

Measuring Civil Society

The WVS measures a respondent's participation in civil society groups in two ways: it asks whether the respondent belongs to certain groups and whether the respondent does unpaid work for any kind of groups. Thus, the survey generated data concerning association membership as well as activism with the association. The survey asks the respondent to identify associations within 14 categories:

1. Social welfare services for elderly, handicapped or deprived people

2. Religious or church organizations
3. Education, arts, music or cultural groups
4. Labor unions
5. Political parties or groups
6. Local community action and issue groups
7. Third-world development or human rights groups
8. Environmental or animal rights groups
9. Professional associations
10. Youth work groups
11. Sports or recreational groups
12. Women's groups
13. Peace movement
14. Voluntary organizations concerned with health

Besides these 14, the survey includes an "Other" category for the respondent to choose. Asking about both membership in and volunteering work for these groups gauges both the passive and active involvement of the respondent. One can belong to a group without actively participating in or supporting the group's work. Thus, a mere measurement of membership does not sufficiently provide information regarding citizens' involvement in civil society.

Unfortunately, this measurement only asks the respondent to report whether she or he belongs to or volunteers for groups within each category. Thus, if one belongs to three groups within the category of education, arts, or music (3), it only counts as one. But if one belongs to one group in category (3) and one group in category (4), then it counts as two. Nonetheless, the survey questionnaire assumes that involvement in multiple groups within one category does not increase the density of civil society as much as involvement with groups of multiple categories (Norris, 2002). In this regard, the survey data still serve a good purpose for our analysis.

Involvement in civil society in the five East Asian societies during the Fourth Wave WVS appears in Table 7.1 and Table 7.2. Taiwan is not included in this chapter's analysis due to inconsistency in data collection: the 1995 survey, for which we have only Taiwan data, does not use the same categories when measuring associational life. As the data show, about half of the people surveyed do *not* belong to or volunteer for any kind of civic groups, although about 15% belong to or volunteer for three or more *kinds* of civil society groups. Among the five societies, Vietnam and South Korea seem to have the most participatory population, while the publics in Singapore and Japan are least active in civil groups. People in China tend to belong to very few (0.39) kinds of groups but are active in a much larger number of groups (1.97).

Table 7.1. Association membership and activism in East Asia.

	Association Membership (number of civil society groups to which one belongs)		*Association Activism (number of civil society groups for which one volunteers)*	
	Frequency	*Percent*	*Frequency*	*Percent*
None	3,862	51.4	3,600	47.9
One	1,773	23.6	1,994	26.5
Two	810	10.8	833	11.1
Three or more	1,067	14.2	1,086	14.5
Total	7,512	100.0	7,512	100.0

Source. WVS, 2000–2001, China, Japan, South Korea, Singapore, and Vietnam.

Table 7.2. Average civil society involvement in East Asia.

	Average Number of Civil Society Categories	
	Association Membership (number of civil society groups to which one belongs)	*Association Activism (number of civil society groups for which one volunteers)*
Japan	.77	.24
S. Korea	1.47	.87
China	.39	1.97
Vietnam	2.30	1.99
Singapore	.83	.57

Source. WVS, 2000–2001, China, Japan, South Korea, Singapore, and Vietnam.

I recoded these two measurements so that "0"–"2" represent the actual number of involvements, while three or more involvements are coded as "3." Then I combined these two measurements to create a new variable that ranges from 0 to 6. The greater the value of this variable means more active involvement in civil society. Table 7.3 shows the distribution of this variable.

Independent and Controlling Variables

Self-Expression Values. These comprise the major independent variable—a factor score of several attitudinal variables calculated within each of the five societies. See chapter 4 for computational analysis of this variable. Tables 4.1 and 4.2 include variables in this factor score.

Life Satisfaction Variables. As a general rule of studying political behaviors, I control individual overall life satisfaction

Table 7.3. Civil society involvement in East Asia.

	Frequency	*Percent*
0	8,921	45.7
1	4,415	22.6
2	2,783	14.3
3	1,938	9.9
4	557	2.9
5	245	1.3
6	656	3.4
Total	19,516	100.0

Source. WVS, 2000–2001, China, Japan, South Korea, Singapore, and Vietnam.

and satisfaction with financial status. Modernization theory of political behaviors (Inglehart, 1997) considers economic status a determinant of an individual's likelihood of participating in leisure, civic, and political actions, and affluence and economic security as necessary for active participation. In the survey, the question "How satisfied are you with the financial situation of your household?" and the question "All things considered, how satisfied are you with your life as a whole these days?" are two measurements used for this purpose. Both are ordinal measurements with a value ranging from 1 to 10.

Attitudinal Variables. Here I assume that specific attitudes affect an individual's behavior. That is, I assume several attitudes are especially important in affecting an individual's degree of involvement in civil society. For example, we naturally assume that people who consider helping or serving others an important part of one's life will more likely participate in groups that aim at poverty relief or welfare work; people who consider religion important will more likely join church-related groups; and people who consider leisure important will more likely join cultural or sports groups. Hence, I control the following attitudinal variables, all ranging from 1 to 4, with the question:

How important is each of the following in your life?

- Friends
- Leisure
- Politics
- Religion
- Service to others

Of course, it also happens that people's involvement in these groups shapes their attitudes, so that people who participate in welfare groups tend to feel more strongly that serving others is important as a result of their experiences performing these works. But our purpose here is not to determine the causal direction of this relation. The purpose of this study is to determine the net effect of self-expression values on civil involvement. Thus, using these attitudinal variables as controlling variables in the analysis should not cause a serious problem related to causal direction.

Age, Gender, College Education, and Countries. Younger people will more likely participate, as will more educated people. For this reason, I control demographic variables: age, gender, and education. To measure education, I use a dichotomous variable concerning whether one has a college education.

Also, to control cross-national difference, I created a dichotomous variable for each of the countries except for South Korea. That is, every country is compared to South Korea.

Regression Results

Table 7.4 contains the results of the regression analysis. Self-expression values, as expected, have a positive and significant effect on civil involvement. The unstandardized regression coefficient is 1.6, which is more than one quarter of the scale of the dependent variable (0-6). Financial satisfaction and life satisfaction also have positive and significant effects on civil involvement, as do several attitudinal variables: politics, religion, and service to others. Males will more likely participate in civil society, and college-educated individuals will more likely participate than others. Younger people are slightly more active than older people, although the difference is only marginally significant (significant at only 0.1 level). Among these countries, China and Vietnam seem to have more active civil involvement than Korea, while people in Japan and Singapore show less activity (i.e., after controlling other factors).

Discussion and Conclusion

The empirical research in this chapter focuses on two important generalizing paths: one path leads through the research of political behavior and the other through democratization. Modernization theorists have focused on explaining changing citizen politics by changed socioeconomic conditions (Barnes & Kaase, 1979; Flanagan & Lee, 2003; Inglehart, 1990; Kaase, 1999). These works argue that affluence and postindustrialization have

Table 7.4. Regression analysis on participation in civil society groups.

Dependent Variable: Civil Society Involvement (0–6)

	Unstandardized Coefficients B	*Standard Error*	*Standardized Coefficients Beta*	*T-value*	*Significance*
Self-expression values	.161	.025	.083	6.502	.000
Financial satisfaction	.034	.013	.040	2.652	.008
Life satisfaction	.049	.014	.054	3.548	.000
Politics important	.128	.030	.057	4.268	.000
Service to others important	.170	.036	.061	4.679	.000
Religion important	.294	.028	.167	10.643	.000
Friends important	.005	.039	.002	.138	.890
Leisure important	.062	.037	.023	1.688	.091

Gender (Male = 1)	.164	.047	.042	3.484	.000
College educated	.267	.066	.053	4.046	.000
Age	–.003	.002	–.022	–1.692	.091
China	.227	.086	.045	2.639	.008
Vietnam	1.130	.079	.233	14.249	.000
Japan	–.727	.085	–.124	–8.525	.000
Singapore	–1.007	.074	–.225	–13.609	.000
(Constant)	3.053	.216		14.150	.000
N			5,847		
R-Square			.182		

Source. World Values Surveys, 2000–2001, China, Japan, South Korea, Singapore, and Vietnam

resulted in a postmaterialist public—one that participates in politics in innovative ways. These theories have largely explained the rise of the so-called New Social Movements (NSM), such as the women rights movement and environmentalism. Thus, while some scholars worry about the decline of social capital (Putnam, 2000), others point to the rising tides of (nontraditional) citizen participation (Catterberg, 2002; Kaase, 1999; Welzel, Inglehart, & Deutsch, 2005).

Three characteristics about this body of research make the current chapter significant. First, existing inquiries have focused largely on contentious forms of citizen engagement: petitions, demonstrations, and other forms of protest (Welzel, Inglehart, & Deutsch, 2005). Civil society engagement, despite the importance it has been attributed, has largely been left out from this analysis. Second, as far as we have research concerning what makes people more likely to join civil society groups, the explanatory factors identified have largely been socioeconomic or demographic ones. For example, researchers have pointed out that the better educated, especially people with managerial or professional backgrounds, will more likely join civil society groups (see, e.g., Norris, 2002). Thus, the findings presented above add one more important dimension to the explanation of citizens' associational engagement and activism. Third, most existing studies concern citizen politics in advanced democracies. Studies of civil society in developing countries have mostly been case studies of small sample sizes. We have seen only limited research such as this chapter's—research based on sound survey data of large samples.

We can make several points concerning the study of democratization. Civil society, especially when envisioned as social capital makes up the infrastructure for successful democracies. While such a role first appeared in advanced democracies (e.g., Italy), after the 1989–1991 wave of democratic transition around the world, scholars of developing democracies have pointed to the importance of civil society for a successful consolidation (Diamond, 1997). Such a view of civil society as mainly contributing to democratic consolidation has been called a "liberal perspective" (Grugel, 2002). On the other hand, for a "radical perspective," civil society is more about the space in which citizen groups develop to challenge the state, to the extent that democratic transition should result from such oppositionist pressures (Gill, 2000). As one author argues, "[t]he critical and oppositional functions of the public spheres of civil society perform irreplaceable functions for democracy" (Young, 1999, as cited in Grugel, 2002).

Civil society groups constantly interact and negotiate with the state, demand just political outcomes for citizens, and protect citizens' rights against the state. But scholars taking the radical perspective have pointed to the role of civil society in mobilizing contentious citizen movements (see, e.g., Gill, 2000). Civil society must rise to oppose a nondemocratic regime. Large-scale labor union movements and the civil disobedience that led to democratization in Korea offer good examples (Han, 2001). To a degree, in some of these writings, civil society is close to, but offers a different rendering of the proletariat class in Marxist terminology—the class that aims at revolutionary change of the political status quo. At the least, these scholars continually stress the importance of political parties in the process of democratic transition. Thus, for them, political parties that aim at the transformation of political order best represent civil society, while indeed whether political parties should count as civil society remains largely a debatable question. In another well-cited study, national parliament is treated as an institution of civil society (Rose & Shin, 2001). I have differentiated civil society networks from social movements or other forms of contentious politics. Thus, in this book the study of protest and the study of civil society have been treated separately in two chapters. Civil society, as it is conceptualized in this chapter, refers to the networks that make up the infrastructure of democracy, a point repeatedly made since de Tocqueville.

Clearly, cultural and sports groups will have very different political implications than human rights or women's groups, for example. Thus, by looking at how different groups interact with the sociopolitical environment under a given state, we can sort out whether some forms of contentious politics will derive from some forms of civil associations, to the extent that an opposition movement can develop, on the one hand, and what kind of civil society groups will provide the civic function of supplementing, supporting, and enhancing the democratic state, on the other. Through such efforts, liberal and radical perspectives can to a degree unite in the same intellectual space. As for what this chapter has presented, we can say for certain that rising self-expression values do lead to more citizens' active involvement in civil society, and as such, enhances the prospect for democracy in these societies.

Take China as an example. As of this writing, the rise of affluence and the expansion of self-expression values have resulted in a very active civil society, especially in the cities. By 2005, the number of registered social groups had exceeded 171,000.[1] This still excludes the unregistered groups, which may include more than 100,000 more. While many of these groups do not directly engage in challenging the state, they do empower citizens in their negotiations with the state and provide protection of human rights and other areas. Meanwhile, they provide fertile ground for cultivating the skills and abilities necessary for citizens' actions toward a more democratic society. In this sense "the People" will usher in democracy in China.

NOTE

1. Statistics released by Zhongguo Minjian Zuozhi Wang (China Civil Organization Web) at http://www.chinanpo.gov.cn/web/index.do, accessed June 2007.

CHAPTER 8

THE COMING OF CRITICAL CITIZENS: SELF-EXPRESSION VALUES AND POLITICAL TRUST IN CHINA*

Central to the study of political regimes, political trust reflects a regime's perceived legitimacy. In new democracies, a high level of political trust may facilitate the consolidation process, while a lack of it may contribute to political instability or a return to authoritarianism. In an authoritarian regime, an accurate measurement of the public's trust in government provides an indication of how strongly the regime holds its grip on the public.

This chapter examines the relationship between self-expression values and political trust. Value change holds a central position in the thesis of the "critical citizen" argument within the study of political trust. The emergence of "critical citizens" (Norris, ed., 1999) within advanced industrial societies has gained widespread research attention. In virtually all economically advanced democracies, declining public trust in government institutions and in politicians has become manifest in recent decades (Pharr & Putnam, 2000). Declining public support for government institutions in advanced democracies has been attributed to the materialist–postmaterialist value shift (Inglehart, 1990). Arguably, long-term economic development and increasing affluence since the 1950s have given rise to a public less deferential to authority and increasingly ready to challenge the government through various protest actions (Norris, 1999a). Observers have called such changing patterns of citizens' interaction with the state "democratic malaise" or "crisis of democracy" (Crozier, Huntington, & Watanuki, 1975).

On the other hand, some authoritarian regimes in the world enjoy a high level of political trust. Intuitively, one might expect to find a low level of political trust in repressive authoritarian societies. But survey data contradict this expectation and indicate that the level of political trust in China remains very high.

This raises serious intellectual and practical questions. Why does an authoritarian regime enjoy a high level of political trust in China? Does this finding simply mean that people cannot—out of fear—express any opinions that authorities might view as critical? As we will demonstrate, this does not seem to be the case. The Chinese public does express fairly strong criticism of some aspects of Chinese society, but they express high levels of confidence in the national government.

Furthermore, these findings contrast strikingly to the widely observed phenomenon of low and declining levels of political trust throughout advanced industrial societies. Although rich democracies enjoy both a higher standard of living and more personal freedom than that available to the average Chinese citizen, the Chinese public expresses higher levels of confidence in government than what we find in most advanced industrial societies. The phenomenon of critical citizens seems absent in China. Why? Let us examine the causes of the high level of public support for the state in China by focusing on the role of economic development. I suggest that economic development enhances public support for the government, but it also—in the long run—leads to value changes that promote critical citizens. My analysis will show that, for now, the regime-enhancing effect of economic development still dominates the regime-eroding effect. True, support for government brought on by the increased level of affluence largely overwhelms the effect of changing values on distrust of government, but the emergence of critical citizens will take place in due course.

Political Trust: Global Trends

The concept of political trust is complex, and we can look at political trust or political support on several levels. At the top level, it concerns citizens' attitudes toward (1) the overall political community, namely the nation of which the citizen is a member. Next, it concerns citizens' attitudes toward (2) the regime, such as democracy; or it concerns citizens' attitudes toward (3) government institutions, such as parliament and government agencies. Finally, it is also about citizens' judgments and the attitudes of (4) political actors, that is, individual politicians (Norris, 1999b).

Such differentiation of political trust is important, both normatively and analytically. Normatively, it is important, for example, that we distinguish trust in the regime itself and trust in government institutions. Thus, although political trust, at the level of institutions, is indeed declining in almost all advanced democracies, support for democratic principles has remained firm (Inglehart, 1999). Citizens can make the important distinction between support for democracy and confidence in government (Klingemann, 2004).

Analytically, the definition of research questions requires such differentiation. Here we will focus on trust in or support for political institutions in China (layer 3 above). If one considers regime change, prevailing levels of satisfaction with the incumbent politicians (layer 4) becomes less important—being interesting only to the extent that it can be a factor that affects trust in institutions. On the other hand, trust in institutions may indicate the level of popular support, and thus the legitimacy, of the overall system. Demand for political reform likely grows when key institutions command low levels of confidence. Support for the political community is an important but separate question, and will not be our analytic focus.

Unless noted otherwise, the term *political trust* refers to citizens' attitudes toward government institutions: the national government, parliament, and political parties. Although political parties are generally not considered government institutions, in the context of China, where there is virtually only one party (the Communist Party), and the party hierarchy dominates the state (thus the term *party-state*), *the* Party is indeed a key government institution. In fact, at every level of the Chinese government, the party secretary is the most powerful official, dominating the government. Consequently, in studying political trust in China, one must include trust in the Party.

Since the 1970s scholars have had concerns about declining public trust in government in Europe, North America, and Japan—a development termed a "crisis of democracy" (Crozier, Huntington, & Watanuki, 1975). This trend has continued into this century. American citizens expressing "a great deal" of confidence in their executive branch has decreased from 42% in 1966 to only 14% percent in 2000, and similar levels of confidence in Congress have fallen from 42% to 13%. At the same time (1976–1996), Japanese citizens have become less and less satisfied with their government, political institutions, and politicians. Almost every West European country reports similar trends. In general, while the collapse of Communism in the late 20th century seemed to herald liberal democracy as the form of government that attracts the most public support, public confidence in government institutions in the world's richest and best-established democracies has reached a record low (Pharr, Putnam, & Dalton, 2000).

If one characterizes this situation in Western democracies as *wan ma qi yin* (ten thousand horses all silent), should we take the situation in China as *yi zhi du xiu* (one single flower blossoming)? In a survey conducted on a national representative sample in China in 1993, 94% of respondents agreed or strongly agreed with the statement that, "We should trust and obey the government, for in the last analysis it serves our interest" (Nathan, 2003). In the same survey, scholars found high proportions of citizens agreed or strongly agreed with statements such as "You can generally trust the people who run our government to do what is right"; "You can generally trust decisions made by the central government"; or "The government can be trusted to do what is right without our having to constantly check on them." A composite index formed by these questions shows the mean of political trust in China at that time was +.80 on a –2 to +2 scale. The authors consider this very high, especially given that this occurred shortly after the government's repression of the prodemocracy movement of 1989 (X. Chen & Shi, 2001). In a more recent survey conducted in rural China between 1999 and 2001, 81% of the respondents expressed "relatively high" or "very high" levels of trust in the central government, while those expressing "relatively low" or "very low" account for less than 4% (Li, 2004).

POLITICAL TRUST IN CHINA: DEFINING THE QUESTION

The 2001 WVS provides another opportunity to examine this question. Our data show political trust in China is indeed very high: 97% of the respondents say they have "A great deal of confidence" or "Quite a lot of confidence" in the national government, while 95% say this concerning the parliament (National People's Congress), and 92% say this concerning the political parties (basically the Communist Party). Trust in the civil service and the police is lower, but still 66% say they have quite a lot or a great deal of confidence in the civil service, and 73% in the police (Table 8.1).

To put this into a global context, few countries around the world show higher level of political trust than this. Figure 8.1 shows a selected number of countries included in the WVS. In response to the question, "How much confidence do you have in the national government?" the Chinese public shows one of the

Table 8.1. Confidence in national political institutions in China, 2001.

Can you tell me how much confidence you have in the following institutions?

	National Government	*National People's Congress*	*The Party*
A great deal of confidence	39.1	33.5	29.5
Quite a lot of confidence	57.6	61.3	63.3
Not very much confidence	3.0	4.3	6.7
No confidence at all	.2	.8	.5
N	1,476	1,427	1,392

Source. WVS, China, 2001. Figures are weighted percentages.

highest levels of confidence among the 27 countries examined here. The confidence level in other major political institutions is similarly high, with trust in parliament ranking fourth highest among the countries surveyed and trust in political parties ranking second highest among these countries.

Is this a problem? As students of regime change, should we be pessimistic because the one-party regime in China still enjoys such a high level of public trust? As comparativists we should sort out the problem of causality. Why is there high level of public trust in government in China? Is it because citizens under an authoritarian regime feel threatened so they cannot express their real distrust? Is it because the regime has been success-

Figure 8.1. Global patterns in political trust.

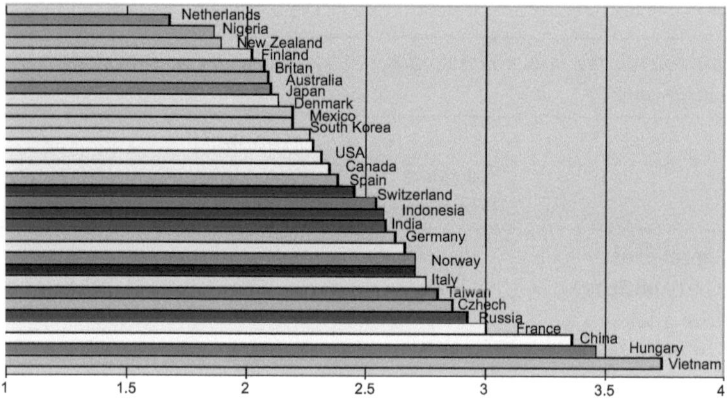

Source. WVS, Waves Three and Four. The respondent is given four choices to the question: How much confidence do you have in the national government? a great deal (1), quite a lot (2), not very much (3), and none at all (4). Data presented here are reverse coded so that 4 equals "a great deal of confidence" and 1, "not at all confident." Country selection criteria: All countries with a confidence level higher than China are included. For countries below China, only the major Western democracies and some developing countries were selected.

ful in propaganda successfully persuading citizens that their government is an excellent one? Is there something intrinsically good about the Chinese political reality that secures genuine public support? Or is it because Chinese society lacks critical citizens?

Fear? Indoctrination?

When we try to determine the causes of high public support for government in China, two potential explanations frequently arise. One is that, in an authoritarian country, the state intimidates its citizens, and, as a result, they cannot express their genuine attitudes toward the government. This we can call the *intimidation hypothesis,*and we can easily test it. If citizens are intimidated by the state, so that they cannot openly voice their distrust, one should find a high and positive correlation between the level of citizen's political fear, on the one hand, and the level of their expressed trust in government, on the other. However, in an earlier study, we have seen that this is not the case. In 1993, it was found, the correlation between political fear and trust in government is very weak, ranging from .04 to .14 (X. Chen & Shi, 2001). Given the general trend of decreasing state penetration and increasing societal autonomy in China in the recent decade (Goldman & MacFarquhar, 1999), it is only plausible that political fear plays an even lighter role in the expressed level of political trust.

Another potential explanation can be called *indoctrination theory.* Such an explanation sees the citizens as immersed in the information generated, managed, and distributed by the state. Researchers find that media does play a role in shaping citizen's attitudes, including trust in government (Miller, Goldenberg, & Erbring, 1979; Robinson, 1976). In these studies people who view contents critical to the government also express lower trust in government. Can we expect that citizens in China show high trust in government because they only receive positive content regarding the government? Without question, a propaganda state, although a weakened one, still exists (Lynch, 1999). Again, this has been found not to be the case. Chen and Shi (2001) found that, around 1993, exposure to media in China actually has a *negative* effect on citizens' trust in government. They thus conclude the propaganda state failed its task of generating public support by its control of information. State monopoly of media, or at least the monopoly of media content, has largely decreased since the early 1990s. Media now cover a large sphere basically free of state intervention, such as entertainment and leisure (Zha, 1995). Under such circumstances, it probably will be even harder to find the direct effect of indoctrination through citizens' consumption of political news.

Economic Performance?

A more reasonable explanation supposes that citizens are indeed satisfied with the performance of government. This is plausible because China has sustained a remarkably high rate of economic growth for more than 2 decades, and the large majority of the populace has benefited from this. True, scholars of advanced democracies have found that decreasing public trust is largely *not* caused by decreased government performance (such as measured by inflation rate and unemployment rate) (Mcallister, 1999). But such a finding does not necessary refute such a linkage between good performance and high political trust. We have strong grounds to believe that high support for government in the 1950s in Germany, Japan, the U.S., and other Western democracies was largely an outcome of good economic performance.

To test whether government performance is the main reason for a high level of political trust, we first need to measure government performance. Precisely, as a study of public attitudes, we should not measure government performance by economic indicators, such as inflation rate or economic growth rate. Rather, we should measure this performance as perceived by the citizens. That is, we should measure an individual's satisfaction with government performance. In the Chinese component of the WVS, two questions are available for this purpose. One asks the respondent how satisfied he or she is with how the people in the national government handle the country's affairs. Another asks the respondent to evaluate the current government as compared with that of 10 years ago. Such questions gauge how citizens perceive the competence of the incumbent government. And in China, most likely the government's performance in the economic and social development fronts determines this judgment. Thus, increased individual well-being will lead to higher satisfaction of the incumbent government and positive assessment of government performance.

Another question can be used to measure government performance. It asks how satisfied the respondent is with the way *democracy* is developing in the country. Although China is not a democracy by any Western definition, the official discourse always maintains that the Chinese people are building a democratic China by continuous political reforms. Such reforms aim at the expansion of political participation of the people and improvement in the government's ability to provide good governance for the people.[1] Thus, this question gauges the respondent's assessment of political reform, whether it is moving toward democracy (meaning, whether they have more political freedoms, more responsive government, and the like, compared to other countries and compared to China of the past). With these data, the performance hypothesis can be tested, as we will see later.

Before Critical Citizens?

As mentioned earlier, the critical citizens theory offers one of the leading explanations for the decline in public support for government (Norris, 1999b). It argues that social and economic modernization give rise to a new political culture conducive to the rise of critical citizens and contentious citizen politics. Industrialization and even more so, postindustrialization bring affluence and the rise of postmaterialist or liberal values. Such values tend to correlate with decreased confidence in public institutions (Inglehart, 1997), and people with postmaterialist values tend to reject authority. This reduces support for the military, government, and other hierarchical institutions (Dalton, 2000; Inglehart, 1999).

The concept of self-expression values and its relationship to democratic politics offers the newest development in this line of inquiry. To reiterate, self-expression values refer to a coherent pattern of value changes taking place in modernizing societies, identified in a long-term effort of scholars observing the dynamics of cultural and political changes (Inglehart & Baker, 2000; Welzel, Inglehart, & Klingemann, 2003). We now know that long-term economic growth and social modernization lead to the rise of values that emphasize political participation and individual liberty relative to material and physical security; a higher level of tolerance toward out-groups; support for gender equality; higher levels of interpersonal trust; and a sense of satisfaction toward life as a whole. This important advance helps in understanding the relationship between socioeconomic, cultural, and political dimensions of human society, an effort we can trace back to the civic culture studies of the 1960s and those that built on it (Almond & Verba, 1963; Pharr & Putnam, 2000).

In China, recent economic development, industrialization, and postindustrialization are leading to the rise of self-expression values (chapters 4 and 5). Given this, why do we not observe a rise of critical citizenship in China? We explain that, although we have seen a rise in self-expression values, its effect on political trust is still marginal. Declining trust in government in Western democracies did not become manifest until the 1970s, after several decades of rapid economic development following World War II. Thus, we would characterize the current situation in China as the era before critical citizens. It is still premature to expect a widespread rise of critical citizens, as the rapid rate of economic development produces high levels of satisfaction among a still predominantly materialist public that has only recently emerged from subsistence-level poverty. For now, economic development still serves to enhance the public's support for government.

Testing the "Before Critical Citizens" Theory

To test this "before critical citizens" hypothesis, I will analyze the impact of economic performance on political trust, on the one hand, and the impact of self-expression values on political trust, on the other. This section explains the methodological design, including measurement of the dependent variable, the hypotheses to test, and the independent and control variables; the next section will present the empirical findings.

Dependent Variable

To measure political trust, I use the average of two indicators: confidence in the national government and confidence in the Party. We will refer to this indicator as "trust in the party-state"; it serves to measure the regime's legitimacy among the public.

Hypotheses and Independent Variables

In my major hypothesis, the before critical citizen hypothesis, for the reasons explained above, I expect that government performance will have a larger impact than self-expression values on citizens' trust in government institutions. Although these values are emerging in China, they are still relatively weak. Several steps will demonstrate the testing of this hypothesis.

A. *Performance Hypothesis*

Economic development results in citizens' high satisfaction with government performance, which in turn leads to high trust in government institutions. We can test this in two steps:

- **A_1:** A citizen's positive assessment of government performance results from increased individual well-being; and,
- **A_2:** A citizen's trust in government institutions results from a positive assessment of government performance.

B. *Critical Citizens Hypothesis*

Citizens with stronger self-expression values tend to distrust government more.

C. *Before Critical Citizens Hypothesis*

The effect of government performance on political trust will largely overwhelm that of self-expression values, thus reducing, if not eliminating, the impact of self-expression values.

The variables used to measure these constructs follow.

Individual Well-Being is measured by the average of an individual's overall financial satisfaction and overall life satisfaction. This averaging results in a variable of overall life and financial satisfaction ranging from 1 to 10. In addition, a variable measures the individual's family financial situation. It asks whether the respondent's family saved money or not during the past year, ranging from 1 to 4. This will gauge the objective financial well-being of the individual.

Evaluation of Government Performance is measured in two ways. The individual's overall satisfaction with the performance of government is an average of two measurements:

> *How satisfied are you with the way the people now in national office are handling the country's affairs? Would you say you are very satisfied (4), fairly satisfied (3), fairly dissatisfied (2) or very dissatisfied (1)?*
>
> *How well are things going in our government compared to 10 years ago? (The respondent is asked to choose a rating from 1 to 10.)*

These two measurements are recoded and combined to a 0-4 scale.

Satisfaction with the Development of Democracy is another variable measuring an individual's evaluation of the incumbents.

On the whole, are you very satisfied (4), rather satisfied (3), not very satisfied (2), or not at all satisfied (1) with the way democracy is developing in our country?

As explained earlier, this measures how satisfied the respondent is with political reform in China.

To test the critical citizen theory, I use self-expression values to measure the value changes that result from socio-economic modernization and the rise of postmaterialism. Self-expression values produce a factor score based on: tolerance of disliked groups (represented by homosexuality), rejection of patriarchal beliefs, rejecting male-centric social relations, democratic aspirations (measuring a preference for liberty and civic rights over material and physical security), and high level of life satisfaction. These variables emphasize liberty and civic rights, tolerance, and life satisfaction. The rise of critical citizens theory predicts that higher self-expression values lead to lower trust in government institutions.[2]

Control Variables

Our analysis will control for age, gender, and educational background, variables thought to have an impact on political trust. We will also control for support of the political community (Klingemann, 1999). We will measure this by asking the respondent how proud she is of being a Chinese, *national pride*. The second, a citizen's psychological involvement with politics, we will measure by a variable of the respondent's *interest in politics*. I also control the impact of state-monopolized information on political trust. Formulated as the respondent's consumption of *political news*, in China this comes exclusively from state-controlled information channels: TV, radio, and newspapers.

EMPIRICAL FINDINGS

Hypothesis A: Performance

Table 8.2 presents the regression analyses by which I test hypothesis A_1 and Table 8.3 that of hypothesis A_2. In Table 8.2, I test economic development on citizens' evaluation of government performance in two aspects: overall incumbent satisfaction and satisfaction with political reform. To measure overall incumbent satisfaction we ask the respondent about her satisfaction with the government now in office, and the current government

Table 8.2. Testing the performance hypothesis: personal well-being and incumbent evaluation.

Dependent Variables:
Model A1.1: Incumbent satisfaction[a]
Model A1.2: Satisfaction with the development of democracy

	Model A1.1	*Model A1.2*
Satisfaction with life and financial status	.091****	.032****
Family financial situation in the past year	.044**	.000
National pride	.130****	.099****
Political interest	.050*	.088****
How often do you follow political news	.084****	.019
Years of formal education	–.038****	–.016****
Gender (male = 1)	.019	–.042
Age groups	–.048**	.017
(Constant)	.56****	3.15****
N	1,153	1,184
R-Square	.156	.104

Source. WVS, 2001.
[a]Satisfaction with incumbent government is an average score of 1) How are people in the national government handling our country's affairs? and 2) How does the current government compare with that of 10 years ago?
*α<.10; **α<.05; ***α<01; ****α<.001.

compared to 10 years ago. Satisfaction with political reform is measured by the respondent's satisfaction with the development of democracy in the country. These are tested in Models A1.1 and A1.2, respectively.

Model A1.1 confirms that improved personal well-being leads to higher satisfaction with the incumbent government. Thus, economic development does lead to positive evaluations of the government. Model A1.2 shows that improved personal well-being makes people more satisfied with the development of democracy in China. This means that a better economic situation also makes people happier with the way government handles political reform in the country. The other findings in these two models come as no surprise. People with higher levels of national pride and people with more interest in politics will more likely give positive evaluations of government performance.

We next test whether positive evaluations of government performance lead to higher political trust. Table 8.3 presents the findings. Two findings are interesting. First, higher levels of personal well-being do not have a direct effect on political trust, as shown by Model A2.1; second, positive evaluations of government performance have strong and significant positive effects on political trust, as shown by Model A2.2. This means that mere economic development is not enough to make people trust the government more. But in so far as economic gains of individuals are attributed to government performance, citizens trust the government more.

As Models A1.1 and A1.2 show, an improved economy encourages people to evaluate government performance positively. We can conclude that economic development drives high political trust in China, in so far as it leads to positive assessment of government performance.

Hypotheses B and C: "Before Critical Citizens"

Model B in Table 4 tests the critical citizens hypothesis. It confirms that people with higher self-expression values tend to

Table 8.3. Testing the performance hypothesis: incumbent evaluation and regime support.

Dependent Variable:
Models A2.1 and A2.2: Political trust—confidence in the party-state

	Model A2.1	*Model A2.2*
Personal Well-Being:		
Satisfaction with life and financial status	.002	
Family financial situation in the past year	.019	
Incumbent Evaluation:		
Satisfaction with the incumbent government		.101****
Satisfaction with development of democracy		.201****
National pride	.149****	.129****
Political interest	.058****	.016
How often do you follow political news?	.019*	.007
Years of formal education	–.024****	–.023****
Gender (male = 1)	.045	.056*
Age groups	.033**	–.032**
(Constant)	3.74****	2.73****
N	1,259	1,033
R-Square	.100	.164

Source. WVS, 2001.
*α<.10; **α<.05; ***α<01; ****α<.001.

distrust government more (with an unstandardized B of –0.035, significant at 0.05 level). The performance effect, as shown in Model C (Table 8.4), however, offsets, if not eliminates, the critical citizen effect.

Table 8.4. Testing the "before critical citizens" hypothesis: self-expression values, incumbent satisfaction, and political trust.

Dependent Variable:
Political trust—confidence in the party-state

	Model B	*Model C*
Self-expression values	–.035**	–.005
Satisfaction with incumbent government		.105****
Satisfaction with development of democracy		.208****
Satisfaction with life and financial status		–.008
National pride	.172****	.021
Political interest	.059****	.021
How often do you follow political news	.008	.014
Years of formal education	–.018***	.005
Gender (male = 1)	.042	.033
Age groups	.005	.014
(Constant)	3.88****	2.86****
N	1,040	878
R-Square	.093	.158

Source. WVS, 2001.
*α<.10; **α<.05; ***α<.01; ****α<.001.

Model C shows that, once we include the positive evaluation of the incumbent government (satisfaction with the incumbent government and satisfaction with development of democracy), the self-expression values variable stops having any significant effect (the B coefficient decreases to next to zero).

Figure 8.2 sums up these findings. Hypothesis A is clearly confirmed. The high level of political trust the regime receives

Figure 8.2. Causal processes for high political trust in China.

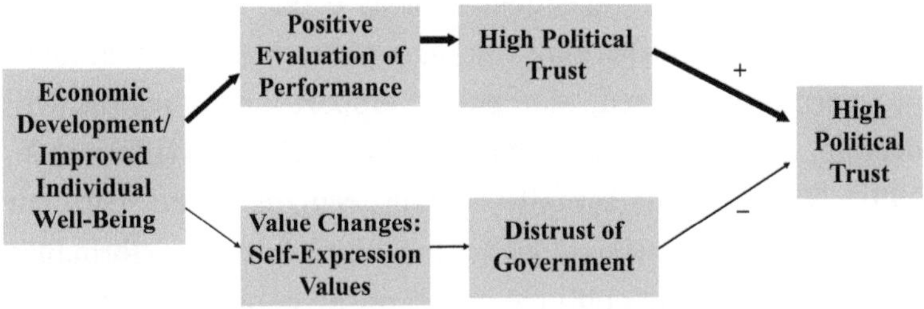

comes largely from citizens' positive assessments of the regime's performance, which reflects improved economic well-being at the individual level, as demonstrated by the causal process depicted on the upper half of the diagram. Hypothesis B is confirmed by the negative impact of self-expression values on political trust, shown on the lower half of the diagram. But this effect of value change is overwhelmed by the effect of performance, in that self-expression values no longer have an impact once we include the performance variables. Two features of the diagram demonstrate this: (1) the causal arrows of the first process are stronger than those of the second process; and (2) when the two processes meet at the right end of the diagram, the effect of critical citizenship is offset by the effect of performance, resulting in high political trust.

Discussion and Conclusion

These findings suggest that the high level of public support the Chinese regime currently enjoys derives largely from its economic performance. This is reminiscent of the way in which the economic miracles of postwar Europe and Japan helped consolidate public support for the governments of these countries. One may speculate that as economic performance deteriorates, or in the long run, as a public emerges that takes prosperity for granted, then public support for the regime will decline, resulting in demands for political change (Huntington, 1991). Whether this actually happens remains to be seen. For the time being, it seems that as long as economic performance remains salient and continues to be positive, public support for the state likely will remain high. In this regard, the diagnosis that a crisis of governance is emerging (Pei, 2002) seems unfounded—at least in so far as mass support is concerned. Nathan's (2003) assessment that this authoritarian regime has demonstrated resilience may be more accurate.

The critical citizens thesis argues that in the long run, high levels of economic development tend to give rise to value changes that result in distrust of government, as well as other hierarchical institutions. It seems that this effect has begun to manifest itself in China, as Model B previously indicated (Table 4.4). Nevertheless, it would be premature to expect a large-scale rise of critical citizens in China. When this phenomenon emerged among the publics of the U.S. and Western Europe in the 1970s, these countries had attained a GDP per capita of about $10,000 USD. Today, the population of China continues moving away from poverty and hunger. By international standards, 5% of the Chinese population still live below the poverty line, and despite the impressive growth in recent decades, GDP per capita (even using the standard of purchasing power parity) still falls short of $3,000 USD.

Needless to say, a society that still places a high priority on economic security will tend to legitimate a regime that can deliver economic development. In the advanced democracies, the growth of a postmaterialist public had, by the early 1980s, reached the point at which postmaterialists were almost as numerous as materialists. In China, our 2001 survey found that about 50% of the Chinese public are materialists, while postmaterialists constituted less than 4%. Under these conditions, economic development tends to enhance, rather than erode, public support for the regime. As Li (2004) puts it, the state still has some breathing room in China.

Performance, What Performance?

Nevertheless, citizens' satisfaction with the speed of political reform (as measured by their satisfaction with the way democracy is developing in their country) also affects the support they give to the regime. Citizens do not look at economic performance alone. For now, Chinese citizens seem still quite satisfied with the way democracy is developing in that country, which seems to indicate relative happiness with the direction and speed of political reform in the country. However, as modernization theorists have demonstrated (Welzel, Inglehart, & Klingemann, 2003), public demands for more political rights and civil liberty tend to increase rapidly once socioeconomic development reaches high levels. On this front, the state may fall short of public expectations relatively soon, particularly if the Party assumes that economic performance will ensure public support and neglects the more formidable task of political reform. Even if the Party realizes the urgency of political reform, its ability to carry it out likely will be much weaker than during periods of economic development. An authoritarian regime likely will fall short in the task of weakening its own control in power.

The Coming of Critical Citizens

My findings do not reject the critical citizens hypothesis, but they do indicate that the impact of this phenomenon is limited to advanced industrial societies. As long as economic performance remains the dominant priority for citizens—and government gets credit for economic performance—the rise of self-expression values does not have a major impact. Nonetheless, the coming of critical citizens will only be a matter of time. As we have seen, rising levels of education tend to make citizens more critical toward government; and self-expression values relate to critical attitudes toward government. Consequently, if socioeconomic development continues in the long term, as it promotes self-expression values and increases education, we would expect the Chinese public to become more critical toward the government. Furthermore, socioeconomic development will reach a stage where prosperity is taken for granted, thus economic performance will not serve to legitimatize the regime's tight grip on power.

Herein lies a dilemma for the Chinese state. Currently, its legitimacy largely depends on economic performance. But socioeconomic development, in the long run, tends to give rise to a public that will more and more question its performance-based legitimacy. As Huntington (1991) has put it: "The legitimacy of an authoritarian regime was also undermined if it did deliver on its promises. By achieving its purpose, it lost its purpose" (pp. 54–55). The rise of critical citizens likely will occur in China and will challenge the state to manage both economic development and public demands for more democratic government institutions.

Notes

* This chapter was originally published in *International Review of Sociology* (IRS), Volume 15, No. 1, pp. 155–171. Permission of IRS is acknowledged.

1. For such an official definition of democracy politics, see the official Party speech delivered at the 16th Party Congress, November 2003.
2. For critical citizens theorists, besides value change, an individual's educational and professional backgrounds and age are important indicators of critical citizenship. That is, younger generations, the better educated, and people employed in the professional or knowledge sectors (law, finance, entertainment, information industries, etc.) will more likely be critical citizens. In this study, I have included education as a control variable, and analysis has shown that education level and self-expression values together already include a large portion of the variation in professional background.

Part IV

Conclusion

Chapter 9

Interpreting the Findings: When Will China Become Democratic?

The previous chapters examined several important questions, including the relationship between socioeconomic modernization and the rise of self-expression values (chapters 4 and 5), the relationship between self-expression values and political behaviors (chapters 6 and 7), and political attitudes (chapter 8). The overarching goal of this study is to understand the dynamics between the three dimensions of human development or the economic, social, and political aspects of modernizing societies. The utmost concern is the establishment, consolidation, and continuous improvement of democratic governance. The central element in this intellectual effort is value change: by observing the public values of a society undergoing socioeconomic modernization, we can understand the strength of demand for democratic political institutions and the social bases for sustaining democracy.

In this chapter, I take the study of value–democratization dynamics a step further. Essentially, I want to propose a time schedule for democratization in a single country—China. This can be done because we are certain of two major linkages: (1) the linkage between socioeconomic development and the level of self-expression strength, and (2) the linkage between the level of self-expression values and the level of democracy. The logical flow of this undertaking is straightforward: probabilistically, because x-level of self-expression values will, in the course of 10–15 years, translate into y-level of democracy, if we know country A's self-expression values at time T, we should be able to predict the level of democracy of A at time $T' = T + 10$ to $T'' = T + 15$.

This chapter is organized in three parts. I first lay out my theoretic bases of predicting the future level of democracy. Then I predict China's level of democracy at around 2010–2015 using China's level of self-expression values for the year 2001. I will also predict China's level of self-expression values for the year 2005, on the basis of which I predict the democracy level of China around 2015–2020.

PREDICTING DEMOCRATIZATION

Huntington (1991) serves as an example of predicting democratization around the world. Based on studies of past democratization cases (the Third Wave from late 1970s through the mid-1980s), he predicted that "Liberalization was under way in the Soviet Union, and quite possibly this would lead to full-scale democratization in Russia" (p. 296). This prediction was not wrong, but it did prove too restrained in light of the actual explosion of democracies in the Soviet Bloc after 1991. Based on his examination of Confucian culture and politics, the role of economy in promoting social changes, and past political developments in East Asia, he was terribly unconfident concerning the democratic future of that region. He saw only Japan and the Philippines as two qualified democracies, and Korea and Taiwan moving in the direction of democracies with "Western form but Asian substance". Concerning economy, he rested his hopes on the possibility of long-term economic stagnation in these countries (China and Singapore most importantly) that would result in popular discontent, which would possibly lead to political changes (Huntington, 1991, pp. 300–306). We can now say, at least by the examples of South Korea, Taiwan, Thailand, and Indonesia, his prediction proved wrong.

Other predicting efforts focus more on the linkage between socioeconomic development and democracy. For example, Rowen uses the projected increases in economic development and education around the world to predict the number of free countries will increase from 61 in 1990 to 74 by 2020, the number of partly free countries will increase from 56 to 77, and the number of not free countries should shrink from 58 to 24 (Rowen, 1995). According to this prediction, by 2020, only 24 countries around the world will be totally nondemocratic. In an more recent effort, he predicts that by 2015, when China's per capita GDP reaches $10,000 (in 1996 purchasing power parity dollars), China will move into Freedom House's partly free category. By 2025, when its per capita GDP reaches $14,000, China will finally become free (Rowen, 2007). Boix and Stokes (2003) found that, excluding oil-rich countries and countries under direct control of the former Soviet Union, when the GDP per capita of a country increases from $1,000 to $12,000, the likelihood of a democratic transition rises 5.5 times. The likelihood of a country's making a transition into democracy is as high as 33% at the GDP per capita level of $12,000 (Boix & Stokes, 2003). According to their prediction, when a country's per capita GDP reaches $4,000, the probability of this country's making a transition into democracy is about 11%. As China's GDP per capita has reached about $6,000 (using PPP calculation) by 2005, using Boix and Stokes' (2003) prediction, the probability of China's making a transition into democracy in any given year is about 15%.

The Prospects of Democracy (Vanhanen, 1997), a much more complicated undertaking in predicting democracy, argues the degree of diversification of material/economic resources determines the pattern of power sharing in a polity. Thus, by calculating a number of indices measuring the degree of resource diversification, one can say whether a polity should be a democracy or not. His main index of resource diversification takes into account factors such as the proportion of urban population, proportion of nonagricultural workforce, adult literacy rate, concentration of farmlands, and others. Examining the data of some 170 countries from 1850 through 1993, he identifies a "cutting point," on the basis of which he then predicts the likelihood of a country's turning into a democracy at a certain point. For East Asia, Vanhanen (1997) predicts that some societies (Indonesia, Japan, South Korea, Malaysia, Mongolia, Myanmar, the Philippines, Singapore, Taiwan, and Thailand) will either turn into democracies soon or will survive as democracies, while some (Cambodia, North Korea, Laos, and Vietnam) will remain nondemocratic for some time to come. For China, the author observes resource diversification increasing due to the modernization of the economy, hence he predicts demand for democratization in China should also increase.[1] Other authors also argue for resource distribution as a key factor in determining political democracy (Boix, 2003).

Inglehart and Welzel's prediction of democracy focuses on the relationship between public demand for and formal supply of democracy (Inglehart & Welzel, 2005). They measure public demand for democracy by the strength of self-expression values, and supply by the degree of democratic governance. The argument goes, if the strength of self-expression values is strong while the level of democracy is low, the political system will change toward democratic governance. For most established democracies (Western Europe and North America), both demand and supply of democracy are high, and these countries are in an equilibrium. For countries with both low demand and low supply, the authoritarian government will sustain power. Around 1990, many countries demonstrated higher demand than supply of democracy, and most of these countries had made the transition into democracy by the mid-1990s or had improved their levels of democracy. These include most of the post-Communist Eastern European countries and countries such as Mexico and Chile. China shows high demand for democracy, while the formal supply of democracy has been very low. The authors predict China will move to democracy in a period of 15 years or less (Inglehart & Welzel, 2005). They do not, however, say why China needs 15 years for democratization to take place.

A SIMPLER BUT MORE FOCUSED PREDICTION

Like Inglehart & Welzel, I predict political change by looking at the strength of self-expression values. In the past chapters, we saw that strong self-expression values at the individual level means higher aspiration for democratic governance. At the societal level, self-expression values indicate public aspiration to liberty, freedom, self-actualization, and political rights. Such aspiration in due course will translate into the political arrangements known as liberal democracy. The exact process of political changes may be difficult to depict, but with the presence of strong public demands, political changes will occur through certain processes.

Measuring Democracy

I use the Freedom House rating of democratic governance to measure the "democraticness" of regimes around the world. This rating system takes into account two dimensions of a political system: the degree of political rights and the degree of civil liberty people under that system enjoy. Freedom in these two dimensions is necessary for a regime to be called a democracy. For example, a democracy should allow both competition for political power and the participation of citizens in the competition (Dahl, 1971). Also, it should further protect citizens' liberty rights, such as free expression (Diamond, 1996). The political rights rating measures both the level of competition and participation of the system, and the civil liberty rating measures the level of civil liberties citizens enjoy under the system.

Each rating ranges from 1 to 7, and political systems around the world are categorized by these ratings. It uses higher values to represent less democratic systems, and lower values for more democratic ones. For each of the two dimensions, a score of 1 to 2 is considered free, 6 to 7 is considered not free, and 3 to 5 is considered partly free. The degree of democratization of a political system is judged by the average of its scores in the two ratings. For example, if country A is rated 3 (partly free) in its political rights, and 5 in its civil liberties, then its overall rating is 4, and the country as a whole is rated as partly free. In 2002, China earned a 7 rating (not free) for its political rights and 6 (not free) for its civil liberties. In that same year the United States earned a 1 (free) for both dimensions.[2]

Given this measurement, I intend to predict the timing for China to move from one category to another (i.e., from not free to partly free, and from partly free to free). Using global data, can we find a level of self-expression values, *V*, that can translate into political changes in the following 10–15 years that will affect a change of a country's categorization? If such a *V* is empirically determined, we can see whether the strength of self-expression values in China is higher or lower than this *V*, and if it is lower, when it will reach that level.

Looking for a Threshold

The availability of two sets of data makes this mission possible. In the last 2 decades, the world witnessed several dozen countries moving from not free to partly free or free. The largest portion of this wave of democratization occurred between 1989 and 1993. By around 2000, it became clear some of these cases consolidated their democratic gains, others suffered reversal to authoritarianism, and yet others continued to struggle with consolidation. This pattern forms the wave of democratization (and dictatorship) that McFaul calls the Fourth Wave (McFaul, 2002).

Thus, it appears we can group the Fourth Wave into two groups, both of which groups contain countries that made the shift away from being not free around 1990. But for one group, by 2000 the countries still struggled with consolidation (i.e., by 2000 they still rated as partly free), while for another, the countries were well consolidated (rated as free). I name the first group the Unfinished Fourth Wave, and the second, the Consolidated Fourth Wave. Table 9.1 shows these countries.

Table 9.1. The same Fourth Wave, different progresses: countries moved from not free to partly free or free, 1989–1994, with some moved to free by 2000.

	Freedom House Ratings					
Nation	*1989*	*1990*	*1995*	*2000*	*Self-Expression*	*Year of Survey*
Consolidated Fourth Wave						
S Africa	11	9	3	3	–0.73	1990
Czech	12	4	3	3	0.18	1990
Lithuania	11	9	3	3	–1.14	1990
Latvia	11	9	4	3	–0.73	1990
Estonia	11	9	4	3	–0.56	1990
Slovakia	12	4	5	3	–0.63	1990
Romania	14	11	7	4	–1.07	1990
Bulgaria	14	7	4	5	–0.87	1990
Mean Self-Expression Values					–0.67	
Unfinished Fourth Wave						
Ghana	11	11	8	6	–1.31	1995
Moldova	11	9	8	6	–1.30	1996
Ukraine	11	9	7	8	–1.06	1996

(continued)

Table 9.1. *(continued)* The same Fourth Wave, different progresses: countries moved from not free to partly free or free, 1989–1994, with some moved to free by 2000.

	Freedom House Ratings					
Nation	*1989*	*1990*	*1995*	*2000*	*Self-Expression*	*Year of Survey*
Georgia	11	9	9	8	–1.35	1996
Armenia	11	9	8	8	–1.32	1997
Albania	14	13	7	9	–1.54	1998
Russia	11	9	7	10	–0.73	1990
Azerbaijan	11	9	12	10	–1.34	1996
Mean Self-Expression Values—Unfinished Fourth Wave					–1.24	
Mean Self-Expression Values—All Fourth Wave					–.95	
China	14	14	14	13	–1.23	2000

Sources. Freedom House Rating (www.freedomhouse.org). The lowest rating for a single country in a single year is 2 (1 and 1 for each of the two dimensions, political rights and civil liberties, respectively), and the highest is 14 (7 and 7 for each of the two dimensions); self-expression values: WVS.

Among the 60-odd societies for which we have at least one wave of WVS data, 16 of them made it to the Fourth Wave of democratization. They moved away from being not free around 1990, and are either free or partly free as of 2000. Half of these 16 countries (rated free in 2000) belong to the Consolidated Fourth Wave (South Africa, Czech, Lithuania, Latvia, Estonia, Slovakia, Romania, and Bulgaria), and another half (rated as partly free in 2000) belong to the unfinished (Ghana, Moldova, Ukraine, Georgia, Armenia, Albania, Russia, and Azerbaijan). Of all the 16 Fourth-Wave societies, around

1990,[3] average self-expression values equaled –.95. This figure for the unfinished group is –1.24, and for the major group –.67. To put these figures into perspective, the average self-expression values of countries rated free in 2000 (mostly European and North American) is 0.32 around 1990, that of those rated partly free is 0.83, and that of not free, –1.11.[4]

Qualifications

We need to make several qualifications. First, the Freedom House rating offers a convenient and logically clear measurement of the level of democracy, and it is widely recognized as an effective instrument—but it has its shortfalls. For example, its rating relies on expert observation. Such a method often generates disputable measurements. Also, its rating often favors countries with elections, sometimes neglecting the quality of elections in some countries. Nonetheless, I take it as an approximate measurement of democracy and, at least for the moment, treat these shortfalls as minor. Second, my selection of cases on which to base the comparisons, the so-called Fourth Wave of democratization, is also strictly defined. For example, countries that were already in the category partly free by 1989—such as Taiwan, India, and Brazil—but made the shift into the category of free around 1989–2000, are not included. But these are also important cases to look at to understand the relationship between social values and democratization. In addition, countries such as Singapore and Malaysia that remained partly free all through the 1980s and 1990s are not included as cases comparable with China. Furthermore, I did not include countries not surveyed by WVS in 1990 or 1995. Thus, countries such as the Kyrgyz Republic, which made the transformation into democracy (and then back to semidemocracy or semiauthoritarianism), are not included. With these methodological limitations in mind, we use our best data available to predict the future of democratization in China.

China at 2020: Democracy at Last?

In any case, this analysis will confirm the correlation between strength of self-expression values and subsequent political development toward a higher level of democracy. In studying the prospect of democracy in China, or in any country, the change in the social values must inform us of the direction in which the overall political changes will lead.

China: 2010–2015

Where did China stand at the year 2001? As Table 9.1 shows, China was rated not free (Freedom House score equals 13). But the strength of self-expression values in 2001 was –1.23, about the average of the unfinished Fourth-Wave countries around 1990 (–1.24). Can we venture to say that during the 10–15 years following 2001, China's rating will move from not free to partly free (between 6 and 10)?

Prediction I

> **Between 2010–2015, China will make the shift from not free to partly free.**

We should note that our analysis cannot determine the exact extent of this change (i.e., whether it will rate as 10, 9, 8, 7, or 6). Given the slow nature of political change in general (barring major crises such as the 1989 political earthquake), however, the Freedom House rating of China in 2010–2015 will likely be near the high end of this spectrum, meaning 10 or 9. We should also note that we cannot determine the exact year this shift will occur.

China: 2015–2020

Let us attempt a further effort at projecting. If we can calculate self-expression values of China at another time, say 2005, then we can predict its level of democracy 10–15 years from that point. We do this by a regression analysis using self-expression value as the dependent variable and socioeconomic indicators as independent variables. We can make a regression model that explains the level of self-expression values using socioeconomic variables 5 years before we measure the time self-expression values.

$$\text{self-expression}_t = a + \sum b_i \text{Socioecoindicator}_{(t-5)i} + \varepsilon \qquad \text{(I)}$$

Formula I illustrates this logic. The strength of self-expression at time t equals the linear function of several socioeconomic development indicators at time $t - 5$. Using our data set, we can conduct a regression analysis for self-expression values around 2000 (i.e., $t = 2000$). After trying out various combinations of socioeconomic indicators,[5] the final regression model appears in Table 9.2.

In this analysis, three socioeconomic indicators serve as independent variables: Gross National Income (GNI) per capita, degree of industrialization (percentage of workforce in industry),

Table 9.2. Socioeconomic development and self-expression values.

*Dependent Variable: Strength of Self-Expression Values Around 2000**

	Unstandardized B	*SE*	*Significance Level*
GNI per capita[a]	.106	.016	.000
Percentage of labor force in industry[b]	–.206	.075	.008
Percentage of labor force in service sector[c]	.214	.066	.002
Constant	–1.225	.307	.000
R-Square			.612
N			78

Source: Self-expression values: WVS.
[a]Data of 5 years before survey are used. Figure in thousands and purchasing power parity.
[b, c]Data of 5 years before survey are used. Both rounded to the closest percentile (meaning, ≤5% = 0, 6–15% = 1, 26–35% = 3, etc.).
Independent variables: World Bank: World Development Indicators.
*For countries surveyed in 2000, the 2000 data is used; for others (about 10 cases), the 1995 data is used.

and degree of postindustrialization (percentage of workforce in service). With this result, formula I is transferred as follows:

$$\begin{aligned} \text{Self-expression} = &- 1.225 + .106{*}\text{GNI/Cap}_{\text{5-yr-earlier}} \\ &- .204{*}\text{Industrialization}_{\text{5-yr-earlier}} \\ &+ .214{*}\text{Post-Industrialization}_{\text{5-yr-earlier}} + \varepsilon \quad \text{(II)} \end{aligned}$$

Without doubt, these choices of variables for the regression models can be subjected to discussion. I included only three:

economic development (GNI per capita), industrializatio, nand postindustrialization. But some other variables may also matter. For example, Inglehart's works have dealt nicely with the "cultural zone" effect (Welzel, Inglehart, & Klingemann, 2003). I have interpreted the regression results without worrying about the probabilistic aspects of this method of analysis. More rigorously, when we predict the strength of self-expression values for a country (in this case, China of 2005) by plugging in the regression models, one should consider the confidence we have in this prediction. That the plugging-in result is *x* only means it is highly like to be *x*. There is, certainly, a probability it will fall within a zone center around *x*.

Nevertheless, this model still modestly serves our purpose to estimate the strength of China's self-expression values in 2005. Next, we only need to plug into formula II the socioeconomic indicators of China for the year 2000. We can obtain these from the appropriate World Development Indicators (World Bank, 2002). China's GNI per capita (purchasing power parity) of 2000 is 3.9 (in thousands), percentage of labor force in industry is 22%, rounded as 2, and percentage of labor force in service is 13%, rounded as 1 (both these figures are for 1998, as more recent ones are not available). With these, we can calculate China's self-expression values level for 2005:

$$\text{Self-expression}_{\text{China2005}} = -1.225 + .106*3.9 - .204*2 + .214*1 = -1.00$$

How significant is this level of self-expression values? (1) It is higher than the Unfinished Fourth Wave, which is –1.23. But,

(2) it is still lower than the Consolidated Fourth Wave, which is –0.67. (3) It is, furthermore, close to the average of all Fourth-Wave countries around 1990, which is –.95 (see Table 9.1) .

Given this strong level of self-expression within Chinese society, we can probably conclude that, during the 10–15 years following 2005, China's political changes will continue in the direction of more democratic governance (based on (1) and (3) of the preceding paragraph). In this period of time, China probably will not be able to move to the free category (based on (2) of the proceeding paragraph). But it is likely that by 2015, it will approach even closer the lower end of the partly free spectrum compared to the year 2010. That is, while Prediction I says around 2010, China's Freedom House rating should be close to 9–10, by around 2015, it should be around 6–8.

This resembles the era when Asian democracies stood at the brink of shifting from partly free to free, such as South Korea in the early 1980s, and Taiwan from the mid-1980s through the first free presidential election of 1996. Although some countries might get trapped in the partly free category for a very long period, more likely the next step after arriving at the lower end of partly free is to move into the free zone (see Appendix). This takes us to

Prediction II

> **Around 2015–2020, China will reach the brink of moving from partly free to free.**

Combining the two predictions, we can probably expect a China in the partly free category between 2010 and 2015, and about to move into the category of free by 2020. Whether democracy will be in place (such as a free national election) depends on how politics evolve. What this means is that during the period of 2015–2020, citizens in China will be ready for and will demand a formal democratic government.

GROWING DEMOCRATS IN CHINA

Many people will consider such a conclusion as too optimistic. Indeed, China of the early 21st century represents a society and polity full of complexities. On the one hand, vast and increasing social inequalities, large-scale popular discontent, formidable economic challenges, and endemic corruption of public officials, all contribute to serious crises of governance—not to mention the peril of a regime collapse (Chang, 2001; Pei, 2002; S. Wang, 2003). On the other hand, the authoritarian regime has demonstrated immense capability and adaptability in governing, so that it has so far largely succeeded in not only regenerating itself, but also in delivering public goods that help it secure sufficient public support (Nathan, 2003; D. Yang, 2004).

But several trends are unmistakable. China's economic growth will sustain, giving rise to a more and more secure and postmaterialism-oriented public. Generations socialized in the postreform era (i.e., cohorts born after the late 1970s) will have much stronger self-expression values. For example, of people born after 1978 (the year China's economic reform started), 31% believe that a national priority should be giving people more say in their jobs or communities, compared to 15% of those born before 1978. Similarly, 54% of the post-1978 population believes that giving people more say in important government decisions should be a national priority, compared to 34% of those born before 1978 (Z. Wang, 2007).

In the 2002 East Asian Barometer (EAB) survey, a few questions gauged individual authoritarian vs. democratic orientation. The interviewee was asked whether she or he agreed with statements such as: citizens should always follow the decisions of government leaders, legislative check of government reduces government efficacy, and too many ways of thinking will make society chaotic. The exact wordings of these statements appear in Table 9.3.

A significant portion of those surveyed rejected the nondemocratic statements. That is the first good news. But more importantly, the postreform generation (18–25 at the time of the survey in 2002) rejected such nondemocratic thinking even more. For every statement, the percentage of rejection among the postreform generation was 10–20% higher than the prereform generations. The biggest difference involved the statement: "If we have political leaders who are morally upright, we can let them decide everything." While 46% of the prereform population rejected such way of thinking, an overwhelming majority, 75%, of the postreform generation rejected it—a difference of almost 30 percentage points. Regarding the statement that government should control free flows of ideas (3), the difference was 22%. The third largest difference was found in statement 2 (we should all follow government decisions), with an 18% difference). On average, the difference between the postreform generation and the prereform population was 15%.

We see in this simple analysis that by the turn of the 21st century, economic growth that started in the late 1970s produced a generation of Chinese citizens that is much more prodemocratic than the rest of the society. At the time of the 2001 WVS and 2002 EAB, this cohort was between 18 and 24 years old (people

Table 9.3. Generational differences in authoritarian vs. democratic orientations.

	Percentage Reject	
	Pre-reform Population %	*Post-reform Population* %
1. You can generally trust the people who run our government to do what is right.	14	25
2. Government leaders are like the head of a family. We should all follow their decisions.	39	57
3. The government should decide whether certain ideas should be allowed to be discussed in society.	36	58
4. When judges decide important cases, they should accept the view of the executive branch.	44	51
5. If the government is constantly checked (i.e., monitored or supervised) by the legislature, it cannot possibly accomplish great things.	57	64
6. If we have political leaders who are morally upright, we can let them decide everything.	46	75
7. If people have too many different ways of thinking, society will be chaotic.	37	48
Average	39	54

Source. East Asian Barometer 2002, China.

younger than 18 were not sampled). As sustained economic growth enables more and more people to live in prosperity, we can expect newer generations to be more prodemocratic than older ones. Hence, the 1980s cohort is more prodemocratic than the 1970s cohort, and the 1990s cohort is more prodemocratic than the 1980s cohort (see also Figure 4.3).

By 2020, these cohorts will fill Chinese society (when the 1970s cohort reaches their 40s). Forty years of continuous economic growth will mean a society as self-expression-oriented as Taiwan and South Korea in the mid-1980s and West Europe in the 1970s. Hence, the trends toward social pluralism, marketization, emerging civil society, and growing outspokenness of the public, will also continue in China. By then, even among the ruling elites, many will embrace self-expression values such as stressing liberty and individual rights. Around 2007–2008, people were already predicting that Chinese leaders around 2020 would be "less ideological and more market-savvy", and they "will have liberal thinking and open minds. They'll see an era of changes" (M. Liu & Ansfield, 2007). If history is our teacher, there is no reason that we should not prepare ourselves to see further liberalization and democratization in a country like this.

As a *Newsweek* article predicted, leaders of China around 2020, as they will be those grew up during the 1980s, "can understand how prosperity helped toppled dictatorships in South Korea and Taiwan" (M. Liu & Ansfield, 2007). In the years leading up to the 2020s, political leadership in China (or in any country with the same conditions) will have to introduce institutional reforms. The better outcome would be that institutional reforms more or less catch the increase in pressure for more political openness. That is, reforms such as a freer press and more open elections at local levels will be introduced in time to meet the expectation of the majority of the populace. Given Predictions I and II earlier, it is likely by 2010, free press will be largely in place, and village elections will also see counterparts in the cities. By 2015–2020, free elections will be seen at the provincial level. That is, China will be short of only a free national election to be categorized as free. The alternative outcome will prove disruptive. It means, among other things, failure to introduce political openness would bring protests in the streets. Both the public and the government do not need to look far away. The first path has been that of Taiwan (Jacobs, 1998), and the second, South Korea (Oh, 1999). On which one of these roads will future developments lead China? I will address this question briefly in chapter 10.

NOTES

1. But the author also finds that the discrepancy between level of democratization and level of resource diversification (IPR) is still not fatal. Thus the conclusion: "[At 1990], the authoritarian system still has chances of survival because important economic resources and the means of violence have remained in the control of the government."
2. Specifications of this rating system are available at Freedom House's website: www.freedomhouse.org. It is also explained in any edition of Freedom House's *Freedom in the World* publication, also available from its website.
3. For those not surveyed in 1990, I used the data of the 1995–1998 survey. The 1995–1998 survey should not be the same as the 1990 survey, but self-expression values surveyed in two waves are highly correlated. For those countries with both waves of survey data, the correlation between the self-expression values of the two waves is 0.93 or higher. Thus, empirically, it should be acceptable to use the 1995–98 data as a substitute for that of 1990.
4. The last category (those rated not free in 2000) should be viewed carefully because only four of them were surveyed in either 1990 or 1995.
5. For socioeconomic factors that may affect the strength of self-expression values, see Inglehart, 1997; Inglehart & Baker, 2000.

Chapter 10

China: Democratization Under a One-Party Regime

This book has examined democratization from the perspective of citizen politics. Overall it argues that with socioeconomic modernization, the public of a society will come to demand open, responsive, and transparent government. Such public demands will help lead political changes toward the direction of democracy. In earlier chapters, I have shown that such demands originate from citizens' changed world views: people growing up and socialized in a prosperous, complex, and dynamic societal environment are self-expression oriented. They value individual liberty, free expression, and social and culture diversity more than people who grow up in rural, static, and underdeveloped social environments. During the last four to five generations, modernizing societies in East Asia have witnessed such dramatic value changes. As demonstrated in chapter 4, a clear rising trend in people's self-expression values takes place in these societies. Although in each of the six societies examined in this study, the value shift from traditional–authoritarian–paternalist outlooks to self-expression values takes place at different points, the timing of this shift shows clear correlation with economic acceleration and social modernization.

Such a shift from traditional–authoritarian–paternalist outlooks to self-expression values has significant political consequences. People with strong self-expression values will more likely express their demand publicly through collective or individual protests (chapter 6). They engage more actively in self-governance in civil society and assert social space against the state (chapter 7). They criticize the government and deem the regime as too slow in introducing democratic reform (chapter 8). Self-expression values, then, serve as an indicator of how strong the demand for democracy is in the society. If the level of demand for democracy grows, as manifested by the increasing strength of self-expression values, we can predict that democratization will take place if given the right conditions. On such theoretical bases, in chapter 9, I use a mathematical model to predict that democratization will take place in China at around 2015–2020.

But if self-expression values (and the latent demand for democracy it harbors) causes democratization, the process of how it causes democratization still needs clarification. So far, I have treated the process of democratization as a black box. I have conceptualized it in this way: *x*-level of self-expression values equals input into the black box, and *y*-level of "democraticness" equals the output of the black box. *How* the black box works is left out. This is determined by the focus of the book. As a study of only one of the social conditions of democratization—that of citizens' attitudes and behavioral patterns—this book aims only to establish the socioeconomic modernization—value change—democratization linkage. Other potential elements in a democratization game are kept out. In this last chapter, however, I will discuss possible political outcomes of an authoritarian regime's facing increasing public pressure to democratize. Democratization may require a long process and for a country as big as China, no one can be sure what will happen in that process. But as self-expression values raise public demand for democracy, political changes will take place in due course.

Peaceful and Disruptive Ways to Democracy

When public demand for democracy grows rapidly, the path to political change has only two possibilities: peaceful and disruptive. In East Asia, two societies—South Korea and Taiwan—offer two different lessons. Both one-party authoritarian regimes were established in the late 1940s or early 1950s, about the same time the current regime in mainland China was established. By the late 1990s, both had transformed into democracies. Increasing demand for political openness from citizens caused such political changes. In the course of 50 years, it appears the two regimes in South Korea and Taiwan had departed from the same place and reached the same destination. The paths they traveled, however, are very different. Taiwan has seen a relatively peaceful democratization, while South Korea underwent a disruptive process. Here I shall give a very short account of these two paths of political evolution from authoritarian rule to democracy.

The Nationalist Party (Koumingtang or KMT) took over Taiwan from Japanese occupation in 1945. Moving away from mainland China in 1949, they set up a one-party state to rule the small island. To legitimatize its rule, however, in the late 1950s the regime began to allow limited elections at the local level. At the time, opposition parties were not allowed. The KMT was very powerful, especially relative to the level of public demand for democracy (Taiwan was still a rural society, with the majority of the population living on subsistence agriculture). The KMT consistently won all the elections at the local level, while elections for national offices were closed and controlled by the regime. From the 1960s, due to surging public demand, especially from the Bensheng (Taiwanese) population,[1] to open the political system, direct elections were expanded to county-level government. Although forming parties remained illegal, the opposition could compete as Dangwai (literarily, *from outside the* KMT *party*) candidates. By the late 1970s, the demand for democratization had reached a point where the Dangwai candidates frequently won local and county elections. Into the 1980s, the regime expanded elections to the provincial level, and in 1987 it legalized the opposition party. Around that time, the opposition Democratic Progress Party (DPP), largely representing the Taiwanese and running on a platform of Taiwan independence, was already winning seats in the national legislature. It won the mayorship of Taipei, the capital, in 1994. In 1996, the country held its first-ever direct presidential. Four years later, in 2000, the DPP won the presidency. Except for several scattered incidents in which opposition leaders were arrested and jailed and a few public protests of limited scale, this represents a relatively steady and peaceful change process, at least compared to that of South Korea.

The story of South Korea should be familiar to the reader by now (see chapter 6). The Korean Republic, formed after World War II, was an independent democracy. But the Korean War handed the Republic to military strongman Lee. Except for a very brief interval between 1960 and 1961, the military dictatorship basically lasted until 1987. Following the economic takeoff and social modernization of the 1960s, demand for democratization grew rapidly. The military regime, however, failed completely to respond to such demands. It tried to strengthen its control by arresting opposition leaders, mercilessly oppressing public demonstrations, and killing and jailing student protesters. Because the stubbornness of the regime frustrated public demands, from 1980 to 1987 South Korea was basically a battlefield, with large- and small-scale protests erupting almost every day and everywhere. In 1987, during the largest demonstration in Korean history, the regime finally gave up and allowed the first direct election of a state president.

Thus, we have a simplified account of the two histories—simplified to crystallize the historical lessons. That is, facing increasing demand for political openness and democratization, a regime has a choice. It can relax political control and introduce democratic processes and institutions, even if in doing so it manipulates the process and delays changes as long as possible. Or, on the other hand, it can choose to stick to power, strengthen control, and determinedly ignore and oppress people's demands. For any authoritarian regime, the first choice is hard to take, but the second is doomed to fail.

Trends in Political Changes in China

At a time of rapid economic development and social change, the status of the regime becomes a major issue for the observer of China's democratic future. Regarding this question, even the best China experts admit confusion. Some signs suggest that the regime maintains relatively stable control. Some observers argue that the regime shows signs of decay and its collapse is imminent. Those arguing the case of regime demise point to, first of all, obstacles to governance in China: social inequality, corruption and power abuse, labor discontent, social dislocation, a poor public health system, and the list goes on. Secondly, even with an apparently prosperous economic front, structural problems are epidemic: incompetent firms, crippled banks, wasteful production, predatory government, slack technology, and energy shortage. Lastly, the regime itself is dead. Meanwhile, these experts argue, the state has lost its ideological appeal and relies only on delivery of economic performance to appeal to the public. Internally it has lost ideological coherence and organizational strength and relies only on a system of patronage to keep from falling apart. The party is over, this side says (Pei, 2002), and China may be trapped by the problems it faces; hence it is going nowhere (Pei, 2006).

Other scholars argue the contrary. Unprecedented economic growth has rapidly modernized the society and elevated people's living standards, thus boosting public confidence in and support for the regime. Not less importantly, the regime has also gone through tremendous transformation. The regime is now more adapted to internal and international realities and can manage the country's complex and dynamic economy (D. Yang, 2004). Institutionalization of a meritocracy, expansion in political participation and consultation, and co-optation of social and economic elites have enhanced its governing capacity. True, it faces daunting challenges, but the regime has determined to take up those challenges. In doing so, we can fairly judge, the regime has proved its ability. The argument would follow that its newly acquired resilience will enable the regime to maintain power in the years to come (Nathan, 2003).

The regime stability argument can point to some supporting evidence. For example, in Chinese society, most citizens are preoccupied with getting and spending; elites are generally proregime; social discontent is quickly addressed or silenced; and opposition movements find no space for survival. Meanwhile, the state still tries to portray itself as indispensable in the nation's drive toward prosperity and national pride. As long as the majority of the Chinese population sees economic development, national power, and social stability as top priorities, the current political arrangement still works. Data from several national surveys indicate this is the status of public sentiment in China (J. Chen, Zhong, & Hillard, 1997; Z. Wang, 2007) [see chapter 8 as well]).

This, however, is clearly changing. The demand for democracy in China is growing with self-expression values. Demand for liberty, freedom, civil rights, and competitive elections has already taken off in China. Our survey data show that more and more Chinese consider protection of free speech and participation in politics as important national priorities (see Table 9.3 in chapter 9). This situation closely resembles what happened during the 1970s in South Korea and Taiwan. In terms of social changes, more than 2 decades of socioeconomic developments have resulted in a China with diverse social groups. A recent study shows that now there exist in Chinese society ten social strata, which form roughly three social classes (Lu, 2001). A diverse society means different social groups will demand participation in the political process, and formal and effective institutions must exist to meet these needs of interest representation and decision making. In coming years, different social groups in China will certainly demand a voice and participation (Zheng, 2004). Democratization, or whatever name we choose for the political changes that lead to more open and participatory systems, is becoming a goal for the Chinese public. Today's public opinion surveys consistently find the majority of Chinese supporting democracy as a form of government. Even among Chinese government officials, the *ganbu* (cadres), the proportion of those supporting democracy and political reform is high and increasing. Indeed, history has put China in position to choose a managed or a disruptive path to democracy, just as it put Taiwan and South Korea there previously.

The Increasingly Assertive Society

In recent years, rising awareness of citizen rights has brought changes leading to constitutionalism and rule of law. In a notable case in 2003 (the Sun Zhigang Case), a college graduate was accidentally killed due to bad government policies at the local level. Citizens, journalists, public intellectuals, and legal scholars rebuked the government for its unreasonable policy and inability to correct misdeeds. It eventually led to the public questioning of the constitutionality of certain government regulations, forcing the government to take corrective action. In a second notable case—the 2003 antidiscrimination case involving a hepatitis B virus (HBV) carrier—more than a thousand people petitioned the National People's Congress for a constitutional review of the government's recruitment policies across the country. As a result, at the end of 2003, the national government ordered the abolition of this and other similar discriminatory policies across all 30-plus provinces. Several similar cases between 2002 to 2006 demonstrated Chinese citizens' increasing willingness (and the ability to mobilize) to challenge government policies.[2] Meanwhile, many citizens protested abusive government officials. In a well-known 2005 case in Taishi Village, Guangdong, a protest escalated into an open conflict between villagers and police.

Of course, in all these cases the success of limiting government power or requesting remedy was partial. Nevertheless, in all of them the government was seriously challenged and curbed by the citizens. It appears, hence, that citizens, especially those educated and versed in legal language, can fight for rights and justice in the face of government power. Increasingly too, they can organize themselves in large scale. Also important, the emergence of attorneys and social activists who advocate for the wronged, gives voice to those who may not have the knowledge or skill to defend their rights themselves. These developments show that the Chinese polity has taken some, albeit small, steps toward constitutionalism, limited government, rule of law, and political openness in general.

Searching for Good Governance

In fact, in today's China two major impetuses drive democratic changes through the Chinese political system. The first, as I've discussed throughout this study, is rising citizen awareness and demand for rights. The second impetus, ironically, is the Party's desire to maintain its legitimacy by delivering good governance. While the first presses the government to introduce more and more reforms that will legalize citizens' rights against the state and thus further limit the state's power, the second propels the Party to adopt political reforms and build institutions that will deliver more law-based, accountable, transparent, and responsive governance.

The Party's search for good governance may indeed gradually allow more and more elements of democracy into China's political system. At least, at the top leadership level, the Party seems seriously committed to building a competent and good government. In recent years, China has experienced frequent social, economic, industrial, environmental, and public health crises. In dealing with these increasingly explosive crises, leaders realize that openness, transparency, and a system of accountability are indispensable. The severe acute respiratory syndrome (SARS) epidemic in early 2003 was a costly lesson on the importance of transparency. In the single year of 2002, industrial accidents (e.g., coal mine collapses and factory explosions) resulted in 14,924 deaths. In 2005 alone, China had 69 coal mine accidents, resulting in a total death toll of 2,671. In 2003, 379 cases of food poisoning occurred, involving 12,876, with 323 deaths. In June 2007, a scandal broke out in Central China's Shanxi Province, when local government failed to prevent some employers from forcing children to work under slavelike conditions (French, 2007). Through such painful lessons, many caused or exacerbated by government failures, top leadership realized the government processes needed more openness and transparency, so as to prevent or better manage such crises. Since 2004, the central government has promulgated several regulations aiming at increasing transparency and accountability of lower-level governments.

The Party's war against corruption offers another example. The Party now understands that transparency is the key to keeping its officials, who number in the hundreds of thousands, honest. It has decided to build a system of financial disclosure for officials: at the National People's Congress in 2005, it made explicit that the Civil Service Law will soon be revised to include such requirements. The national auditing agency is also empowered to check (and release) financial records of government agencies. In 2004 alone, the National Auditing Authority revealed illegal financial practices of 38 central government agencies, involving a total amount of RMB 9 billion (US$ 1.1 billion). Another practice for more openness and transparency subjects officials to public scrutiny and invites input from citizens. For example, major government appointments are announced for public scrutiny and public hearing sessions are held for some major policy decisions.

To institutionalize transparency, accountability, and openness, the Party has announced that China should build a law-based government (法治政府, *fazhizhengfu*). The impersonal, generalist rule of law should replace the case-by-case handling of corruption or ideological campaign, two methods that the Party used heavily. In early 2004, the government issued a blueprint for building a "government based on rule of law." It emphasized "using legal means in the administration of state affairs, economic, cultural, and social affairs." Most notably, it puts forward concepts such as constitutionality, due process, openness, public right to government information, public right to participation in policy decisions, and citizens' rights to legal remedy. Legal remedy occurred in a well-publicized 2005 case: She Xianglin, a peasant mistakenly convicted of murder and imprisoned for many years, received 900,000 Chinese Yuan (about US $111,000) in state compensation.

Other concrete actions are being taken to achieve governmental goals in accordance with law. For example, a 2005 Law on Legislation was adopted as a legislative check on lawmaking. In addition to asserting constitutionality for any laws and rules of the government, it mandates that only the NPC (National People's Congress) and no other government body can make laws or regulations curbing civil liberty. The Government Force Law (2005), Government Permission Law (2003), and Government Punishment Law (1996) form a relatively comprehensive legal framework limiting government power.

Growing Democracy Under a One-Party Regime?

Assuming the ruling CCP will stay in power for some time, how will democracy come about within such a strong one-party framework? For a long time to come, political changes in China will still come gradually, without fundamentally challenging the Party's power. But nevertheless, this does not mean that there is no hope for democracy. On the one hand, the Chinese society is far more dynamic compared to 20 or even 10 years ago, and it will continue to become more dynamic. A dynamic society demands an open political system. Citizens have become more active, articulate, assertive, and better organized. They represent the real force that will drive the one-party regime to adapt to change. On the other hand, the Party is also consciously reforming the state apparatus to meet the demand of governance. This effort includes reforming obsolete party-state institutions, but more importantly it includes building new ways, with transparency, accountability, representation, and rule of law. Hence, today

China's democratization is not a transition into democracy per se, but should be more accurately characterized as building a democracy from within. In the decade to come, it will be a one-party regime acquiring more and more democratic elements, a form of "democratic growth" indeed. Such a democratic-growth period will last long enough, until the one-party framework itself gradually becomes obsolete. By then a transition into a multiparty competitive democracy becomes possible.

The Hybrid Regime as a Pathway to Democracy

A major theoretical development in the empirical studies of democracy is the concept of "hybrid regime" (Diamond, 2002)—a realization that came after the apparent victory of Western-style liberal democracy at the end of Cold War. Scholars and practitioners realized that the end of authoritarianism does not necessarily mean democracy (Carothers, 2002). Many regimes in the world today, this line of thinking goes, are neither democratic nor strictly authoritarian. They are, in fact, hybrid regimes. Furthermore, people argue that hybrid regimes may be stable, meaning such regimes will not necessarily become democracies. Scholars have used many terms to describe the most important characteristics of hybrid regimes, such as semiauthoritarianism, competitive authoritarianism, electoral authoritarianism, liberalized autocracy, semidemocracy, pseudodemocracy, illiberal democracy, electoral democracy, and election without democracy—"democracies with adjectives" or "adjective authoritarianism." Whatever the name, these regimes all have limited elections, but the system is far from democratic in that either one dictator or one party continuously holds power through oppression or election fraud.[3]

A hybrid regime has three possible courses: remaining stable, reverting to authoritarianism, or moving to democracy. Here I inject my argument: when public demand for democracy is high, a hybrid regime will move to a democracy. Indeed, in modernizing countries, such as China, Vietnam, Singapore, South Korea, and Taiwan, a hybrid regime forms only a middle stage between the strictly authoritarian regime and democracy. In fact, this is not a new argument. Scholars have pointed out that establishment and consolidation of democracy depends on the relationship between demand for and supply of democracy. In post-Communist Eastern Europe and Central Asia, countries with high public demand for democracy have seen democracy consolidated, while those with low demand have seen a reversal to authoritarianism (Ottaway, 2002; Rose & Shin, 2001). Inglehart and Welzel (2005) have convincingly established this linkage at the global level, using cross-national data of public values and democratic governance in more than 80 societies. For those countries where supply for democracy lags far behind public demand, such as China, they argue that transition to democracy will follow suit in a shorter period of time.

How will China evolve into a hybrid regime? In the foreseeable future, the Party will not tolerate organized opposition movements. As a result, no genuine multiparty competition will emerge in the short run. Nevertheless, if the regime introduces meaningful elections, such as the election to provincial assemblies, then it can become a hybrid regime. Once such steps of institutional reforms are taken, the trend toward more participation and less party control will become difficult to reverse.

As mentioned above, in the case of Taiwan, the opposition party first competed as a *dangwai* force and won seats to various elected bodies. In due course, the state has to legalize opposition parties and begin the transition from hybrid to democratic regime.

Recent scholarship seems to suggest such a trajectory of democratization in China. On the one hand, some analyses on global data show that for a country like China enjoying rapid economic development and social modernization, the likelihood of democratization increases with the level of economic development (Boix & Stokes, 2003). Using global data that covers 80% of world population, Inglehart and Welzel (2005) argue that human development eventually means the expansion of human freedom and the institutionalization of human freedom in the form of liberal democracy, a process of which China is not an exception (Inglehart & Welzel, 2005). Rowen's analysis specifically puts China within the global pattern of democratic changes, and predicts that China will move to Freedom House's party free category in the year 2015, and the free category by around 2025 (Rowen, 2007). Indeed, scholarship on political changes within China also points to continuing liberalization. According to Zheng Yongnian (2004), increased public demand for political opening, voice, and participation, will cause the state to engineer a transformation. In engineering such a transformation, Zheng (2004) argues, the state can either seek its sole domination, ally with the capitalist class, or ally with the working class and peasants. Using a game-theory model, Zheng argues that the model of state leading the change, but with participation by the working class and peasants, will be most acceptable to the state and the public. In another study,

Chinese scholars argue that the process of political evolution will first be dominated by state direction, and then it will be followed by state and society collaboration (He, 2004; Kang, 2002). Eventually, however, it will be dominated by societal initiatives. Both studies seem to agree that, although the state will dominate the process of political change at the beginning, with the growth of strength of the civil society, the transformation process will eventually be determined by participation of various social forces.

CONCLUSION

At the close of this study, China teeters on the brink of becoming a hybrid regime. Elections at the village level are conducted in almost 90% of its counties. The Party, as discussed earlier, appears to be seriously considering expanding elections. Delegates to county-level legislatures are now directly elected, although the Party is still studying what powers the legislatures at various levels (county, province, and national) should have. One thing is clear: if the Party is convinced that limited elections will not seriously erode its control of power, it will move to adopt it because it knows elections will give it the legitimacy it desperately needs. It is clear that the Party is carefully studying the successful one-party rule in places such as Singapore and Japan and failed one-party rule in places such as Taiwan. In a word, the Chinese Communist Party plans to introduce elections, while maintaining its control of power—a typical hybrid regime plan.

In chapter 9 I argued that by 2010–2015, China will move from Freedom House's not free category to the partly free category.

Following 2012 (the 18th Party Congress), the Party will open elections, presumably up to the provincial level. The Party will certainly design the electoral system so that it maintains majority in the important elected bodies. Such electoral arrangements may enable the Party to hold on to power for another 10 years or more, as the ruling parties in Taiwan and South Korea (and many other countries) did. But what the Party does not foresee at the moment is, once it institutionalizes elections, it will set itself on the irreversible road to democracy.

This is so because, as argued throughout this study, public demand for democracy continues to grow. Such demand has resulted in the regime's planning to introduce limited elections, hence the upcoming transition to a hybrid regime. Such demand, by the time limited elections are in place, will keep mounting pressure on the regime to continue to open up. While Chinese politics slogs toward constitutionalism, rule of law, transparency, and civil liberties, Western observations (such as those made by Freedom House) are normally tainted by an election bias. Because elections in China are still preliminary, other aspects of democratization in China are insufficiently registered. Freedom House currently rates the situation of political rights in China at 7, while that of civil liberties rates a 6. Combined, this gives China a rating of 6.5, putting China in the nonfree category. But China is clearly different from "politically closed systems," such as North Korea and Iraq under Saddam. The political rights rating of China by Freedom House should change to 6 and that of civil liberties to 5, making China's combined rating 5.5, which would move it into the partly free category. By then we could say that China officially qualifies as a hybrid regime.

As public demand for democracy continues growing strong in China, a hybrid regime will more likely provide the pathway to democracy instead of a condition of prolonged political uncertainties. Hence, in chapter 9, I argued that by 2015–2020, China should be close to moving from partly free to free. In any case, social changes in China have prepared conditions favorable to a transformation out of authoritarianism and toward a more open and democratic system; studies in global democratization support such an assessment. Responding to the doubts that economic development and social modernization may not lead to political changes in China, Dali Yang argues, "Unless skeptics of theory think that the people in the People's Republic of China are of a different species, the doubters cannot simply dismiss the development–democracy relationship." (D. L. Yang, 2007, pp. 60–61).

This book proves that China is no exception to the general pattern: socioeconomic modernization in China (and the other societies included in this study) has given rise to a populace that will come to demand democratic reforms. Such reforms, indeed, have already taken place in incremental ways. As citizens come to demand democracy, they will win it.

Notes

1. The majority (about 98%) of the population of Taiwan are Chinese. One group consists of those settled in Taiwan from the mainland in the course of several hundred years after the Ming Dynasty (1368–1644). In 1949, a huge number of mainlanders moved to Taiwan with the Nationalist government. Since then, those settling in Taiwan before 1949 have been known as Bensheng Ren (the people of "this" province, i.e., Taiwan), and the people who moved to Taiwan in 1949 are known as Waisheng Ren (the people of "other" provinces, i.e. from the mainland). In English, the Bensheng group is called the Taiwanese, while the Waisheng group is called Chinese or Mainlanders. Both groups, however, are mostly Han Chinese. As of 2004, the Bensheng (Taiwanese) group account for 84% of Taiwan's population, and the Waisheng (Mainland) group account for 14% (figures from the CIA World Fact Book).
2. Such as the BMW Case in Heilongjiang Province in which a driver in a BMW hit a peasant woman; the Nujiang River case in which citizens mobilized to stop a dam project; and the high-speed rail case in which citizens demanded the government change course in contracting out a megarail project linking Beijing and Shanghai.
3. See the symposium on "Election without Democracy," Volume 13, no. 2, *Journal of Democracy,* 2002.

APPENDIX

Freedom House Rating for Selected East Asian Countries, 1972–2000 (Shaded areas show the "partly free" periods: Dark grey areas represent ratings between 9–10, and light grey areas, 6–8)

Year	Indonesia	Korea, S.	Malaysia	Philippines	Singapore	Taiwan	Thailand
1972–73	5,5,PF	5,6,NF	2,3,F	4,6,PF	5,5,PF	6,5,NF	7,5,NF
1973–74	5,5,PF	4,6,PF	2,3,F	5,5,PF	5,5,PF	6,5,NF	6,3,PF
1974–75	5,5,PF	5,6,PF	3,3,PF	5,5,PF	5,5,PF	6,5,NF	5,3,PF
1975–76	5,5,PF	5,5,PF	3,4,PF	5,5,PF	5,5,PF	6,5,NF	2,3,F
1976–77	5,5,PF	5,6,NF	3,4,PF	5,5,PF	5,5,PF	5,5,PF	6,6,NF
1977–78	5,5,PF	5,5,PF	3,4,PF	5,5,PF	5,5,PF	5,4,PF	6,5,NF
1978–79	5,5,PF	5,5,PF	3,3,PF	5,5,PF	5,5,PF	5,4,PF	6,4,PF
1979–80	5,5,PF	4,5,PF	3,4,PF	5,5,PF	5,5,PF	5,5,PF	4,3,PF
1980–81	5,5,PF	5,6,PF	3,4,PF	5,5,PF	5,5,PF	5,6,PF	3,4,PF
1981–82	5,5,PF	5,6,PF	3,4,PF	5,5,PF	4,5,PF	5,5,PF	3,4,PF
1982–83	5,5,PF	5,6,PF	3,4,PF	5,4,PF	4,5,PF	5,5,PF	3,4,PF
1983–84	5,5,PF	5,6,PF	3,4,PF	5,5,PF	4,5,PF	5,5,PF	3,4,PF
1984–85	5,6,PF	5,5,PF	3,5,PF	4,4,PF	4,5,PF	5,5,PF	3,4,PF
1985–86	5,6,PF	4,5,PF	3,5,PF	4,3,PF	4,5,PF	5,5,PF	3,4,PF
1986–87	5,6,PF	4,5,PF	3,5,PF	4,2,PF	4,5,PF	5,5,PF	3,3,PF
1987–88	5,6,PF	4,4,PF	3,5,PF	2,2,F	4,5,PF	5,4,PF	3,3,PF
1988–89	5,5,PF	2,3,F	4,5,PF	2,3,F	4,5,PF	5,3,PF	3,3,PF
1989–90	5,5,PF	2,3,F	5,4,PF	2,3,F	4,4,PF	4,3,PF	2,3,F
1990–91	6,5,PF	2,3,F	5,4,PF	3,3,PF	4,4,PF	3,3,PF	2,3,F
1991–92	6,5,PF	2,3,F	5,4,PF	3,3,PF	4,4,PF	5,5,PF	6,4,PF
1992–93	6,5,PF	2,3,F	5,4,PF	3,3,PF	4,5,PF	3,3,PF	3,4,PF
1993–94	7,6,NF	2,2,F	4,5,PF	3,4,PF	5,5,PF	4,4,PF	3,5,PF
1994–95	7,6,NF	2,2,F	4,5,PF	3,4,PF	5,5,PF	3,3,PF	3,5,PF
1995–96	7,6,NF	2,2,F	4,5,PF	2,4,PF	5,5,PF	3,3,PF	3,4,PF
1996–97	7,5,NF	2,2,F	4,5,PF	2,3,F	4,5,PF	2,2,F	3,3,PF
1997–98	7,5,NF	2,2,F	4,5,PF	2,3,F	5,5,PF	2,2,F	3,3,PF
1998–99	6,4,PF	2,2,F	5,5,PF	2,3,F	5,5,PF	2,2,F	2,3,F
1999–00	4,4,PF	2,2,F	5,5,PF	2,3,F	5,5,PF	2,2,F	2,3,F

Bibliography

Abramson, P. R., & Inglehart, R. (1995). *Value change in global perspective*. Ann Arbor: University of Michigan Press.

Almond, G. A., & Verba, S. (1963). *The civic culture: Political attitudes and democracy in five nations*. Princeton, NJ: Princeton University Press.

Astin, A. W. (1984). Student involvement: A developmental theory for higher education. *Journal of College Student Personnel, 25*, 297–308.

Astin, A. W., & Sax, L. J. (1998). How undergraduates are affected by service participation. *Journal of College Student Development, 39*(3), 251–263.

Atienza, J. (1994). An alternative framework for social change. *Intersect, 8*(4–5), 4–6.

Barnes, S., & Kaase, M. (Eds.). (1979). *Political action: Mass participation in five Western societies*. Thousand Oaks, CA: Sage.

Bellin, E. R. (2000). Contingent democrats: Industrialists, labor, and democratization in late-developing countries. *World Politics, 52*(2), 175–205.

Blankenau, W. F., & Simpson, N. B. (2004). Public education expenditures and growth. *Journal of Development Economics, 73*, 583–605.

Bloom, A. D. (1990). *Giants and dwarfs: Essays, 1960–1990*. New York: Simon and Schuster.

Boix, C. (2003). *Democracy and redistribution*. New York: Cambridge University Press.

Boix, C., & Stokes, S. C. (2003). Endogenous democratization. *World Politics, 55*(3), 517–549.

Boussard, C. (2003). *Crafting democracy: Civil society in post-transition Honduras*. Unpublished manuscript, Lund, Sweden: Lund University.

Branson, M. S., & Quigley, C. N. (1998). *The role of civic education*. Washington, DC: Communitarian Network.

Brooke, J. (2003, September 16). Farming is Korean's life and he ends it in despair. *New York Times,* p. A6.

Brzezinski, Z. (2001). The primacy of history and culture. *Journal of Democracy, 12*(4), 20–26.

Carothers, T. (2002). The end of the transition paradigm. *Journal of Democracy, 13*(1), 5–21.

Catterberg, G. (2002). *Transitions to democracy: The post-honeymoon decline of participation.* Unpublished manuscript, Ann Arbor: University of Michigan.

Chan, J. (1998). Asian values and human rights: An alternative view. In L. J. Diamond & M. F. Plattner (Eds.), *Democracy in East Asia* (pp. 28–41). Baltimore: The John Hopkins University Press.

Chang, G. G. (2001). *The coming collapse of China* (1st ed.). New York: Random House.

Chen, J., Zhong, Y., & Hillard, J. W. (1997). The level and sources of popular support for China's current political regime. *Communist and Post-Communist Studies, 30*, 45–64.

Chen, X., & Shi, T. (2001). Media effects on political confidence and trust in the People's Republic of China in the post-Tiananmen period. *East Asia, 19*(3), 84–118.

Chu, Y.-H., Diamond, L. J., & Shin, D. C. (2001). Halting progress in Korea and Taiwan. *Journal of Democracy, 12*(1), 122–136.

Couto, R., & Guthrie, C. S. (1999). *Making democracy work better: Mediating structures, social capital, and the democratic prospect.* Chapel Hill: University of North Carolina Press.

Crozier, M., Huntington, S. P., & Watanuki, J. (1975). *The crisis of democracy.* New York: New York University Press.

Dahl, R. A. (1971). *Polyarchy: Participation and opposition.* New Haven, CT: Yale University Press.

Dalton, R. J. (2000). Value change and democracy. In S. J. Pharr & R. D. Putnam (Eds.), *Disaffected democracies* (pp. 252–269). Princeton, NJ: Princeton University Press.

Dalton, R. J., & Ong, N.-N. T. (2003). Authority orientations and political values in East Asia: A test of the "Asian Values" Hypothesis. *Paper presented at the 2003 annual meetings of the Midwest Political Science Association, Chicago, April 3–4.*

Dalton, R. J., Pham, M. H., Pham, T. N., & Ong, N.-N. T. (2003). Social relations and social capital in Vietnam: Findings from the 2001 World Values Survey. In R. Inglehart (Ed.) (pp. 140–156).

Dalton, R. J., & Shin, D. C. (2003). *Democratic aspirations and democratic ideals: Citizen orientations toward democracy in East Asia.* Unpublished manuscript, Irvine, CA.

de Mesquita, B. B., & Downs, G. W. (2005). Development and democracy. *Foreign Affairs, 84*(5), 77–86.

Delli Carpini, M. X., & Keeter, S. (1996). *What Americans know about politics and why it matters*. New Haven, CN: Yale University Press.

Deutsch, K. W. (1961). Social mobilization and political development. *American Political Science Review, 55*, 493–514.

Diamond, L. (1996). Is the Third Wave over? *Journal of Democracy, 7*(3), 20–37.

Diamond, L. (2002). Thinking about hybrid regimes. *Journal of Democracy, 13*(2), 21–35.

Diamond, L. (Ed.). (1997). *Consolidating the Third Wave democracies.* Baltimore: Johns Hopkins University Press.

Doolin, D. J., & Ridley, C. P. (1968). *The genesis of a model citizen in communist China: Translation and analysis of selected Chinese Communist elementary school readers.*

Fish, M. S. (1998). Mongolia: Democracy without prerequsites. *Journal of Democracy, 9*(3), 127–141.

Flanagan, S. C., & Lee, A.-R. (2000). Value change and democratic reform in Japan and Korea. *Comparative Political Studies, 33*(5), 626–659.

Flanagan, S. C., & Lee, A.-R. (2003). The new politics, culture wars, and the authoritarian–libertarian value change in advanced industrial democracies. *Comparative Political Studies, 36*(3), 235–270.

French, H. W. (2007, June 18). Ideals and reality conflict on Chinese child labor. *New York Times*.

Friedman, E. (1994). *The politics of democratization*. Boulder, CO: Westview Press.

Fukuyama, F. (1995). *Trust: Social virtues and the creation of prosperity*. New York: Free Press.

Galston, W. A. (2001). Political knowledge, political engagement, and civic education. *Annual Review of Political Science, 4*, 217–234.

Geremek, B. (1996). Civil society: Then and now. In L. J. Diamond & M. F. Plattner (Eds.), *The global resurgence of democracy* (2nd ed., pp. 241–250). Baltimore: The Johns Hopkins University Press.

Gibbins, J. R. (Ed.). (1989). *Contemporary political culture: Politics in a postmodern age*. London; Newbury Park, CA: Sage.

Gibson, J. L. (1996). *Putting up with fellow Russians: Political tolerance in a fledging democracy*. Glasgow, Scotland: Centre for the Study of Public Policy, University of Strathclyde.

Gibson, J. L. (2001). Social networks, civil society, and the prospects for consolidating Russia's democratic transition. *American Journal of Political Science, 45*(1), 51–68.

Gill, G. J. (2000). *The dynamics of democratization: Elites, civil society, and the transition process*. New York: St. Martin's Press.

Gilliom, M. E. (1978). Citizenship education in the People's Republic of China. *Theory into Practice, 17*(5), 389–395.

Goldman, M., & MacFarquhar, R. (1999). Dynamic economy, declining party-state. In M. Goldman & R. MacFarquhar (Eds.), *The paradox of China's post-Mao reforms* (pp. 3–29). Cambridge, MA: Harvard University Press.

Grugel, J. (2002). *Democratization : A critical introduction*. Houndmills, Basingstoke, Hampshire; New York: Palgrave.

Haggard, S. (1990). *Pathways from the periphery: The politics of growth in the newly industrializing countries*. Ithaca, NY: Cornell University Press.

Han, S.-J. (2001). Modernization and the rise of civil society: The role of the "Middling Grassroots" for democratization in Korea. *Human Studies, 24*(1–2), 113–132.

Havel, V., et al. (1985). *The power of the powerless: Citizens against the state in Central Eastern Europe*. London: Hutchinson.

Haynes, J. (2001). *Democracy in the developing world: Africa, Asia, Latin America and the Middle East*. Cambridge, UK: Polity.

He, Z. (2004). Jianjin zhengzhi gaige yu minzhu zhuanxing [Incremental political reform and democratic transition]. *Journal of Beijing Institute of Administration* (3–4).

Heng, H. K. (1997). Economic development and political change: The democratization process in Singapore. In A. Laothamatas (Ed.), *Democratization in Southeast and East Asia* (pp. 113–140). Singapore: Institute of Southeast Asian Studies.

Heryanto, A., & Mandal, S. K. (2003). *Challenging authoritarianism in Southeast Asia: Comparing Indonesia and Malaysia*. New York: Routledge.

Ho, M.-S. (2003). The politics of anti-nuclear protest in Taiwan: A case of party-dependent movement (1980–2000). *Modern Asian Studies, 37*(3), 683–708.

Hobsbawm, E. J. (1962). *The age of revolution, 1789–1848*. New York: New American Library.

Hu, S. (2000). *Explaining Chinese democratization*. Westport, CN: Praeger Publishing.

Huntington, S. P. (1991). *The Third Wave: Democratization in the late twentieth century*. Norman: University of Oklahoma Press.

Huntington, S. P., & Nelson, J. M. (1976). *No easy choice: Political participation in developing countries*. Cambridge, MA: Harvard University Press.

Inglehart, R. (1977). *The silent revolution: Changing values and political styles among Western publics*. Princeton, NJ: Princeton University Press.

Inglehart, R. (1988). The renaissance of political culture. *The American Political Science Review, 82*(4), 1203–1230.

Inglehart, R. (1990). *Culture shift in advanced industrial society*. Princeton, NJ: Princeton University Press.

Inglehart, R. (1997). *Modernization and postmodernization: Cultural, economic, and political change in 43 societies*. Princeton, NJ: Princeton University Press.

Inglehart, R. (1999). Postmodernization erodes respect for authority, but increases support for democracy. In P. Norris (Ed.), *Critical citizens* (pp. 236–256). Oxford, UK: Oxford University Press.

Inglehart, R. (2003a). How solid is mass support for democracy—And how can we measure it? *PS Political Science & Politics*, 51–57.

Inglehart, R. (Ed.). (2003b). *Human values and social change: Findings from the World Value Surveys*. Boston: Brill.

Inglehart, R., & Abramson, P. R. (1994). Economic security and value change. *The American Political Science Review, 88*(2), 336–354.

Inglehart, R., & Baker, W. E. (2000). Modernization, culture change, and the persistence of traditional values. *American Sociological Review, 65*, 19–51.

Inglehart, R., & Norris, P. (2003). *Rising tide: Gender equality and cultural change around the world.* Cambridge, UK: Cambridge University Press.

Inglehart, R., & Norris, P. (2004). *Sacred and secular: Religion and politics worldwide*. Cambridge, UK: Cambridge University Press.

Inglehart, R., & Welzel, C. (2005). *Modernization, cultural change, and democracy: The human development sequence*. New York: Cambridge University Press.

Inkeles, A. (1966). The modernization of man. In M. Weiner (Ed.), *Modernization* (pp. 138–152). New York: Basic Books.

Jacobs, J. B. (1998). *Democratisation in Taiwan*. Clayton, Vic: Monash Asia Institute.

Javeline, D. (2003). *Protest and the politics of blame: The Russian response to unpaid wages*. Ann Arbor: University of Michigan Press.

Jennings, M. K., & Niemi, R. G. (1974). *The political character of adolescence: The influence of families and schools*. Princeton, NJ: Princeton University Press.

Johnson, C. A. (1982). *MITI and the Japanese miracle: The growth of industrial policy, 1925–1975*. Stanford, CA: Stanford University Press.

Kaase, M. (1999). Interpersonal trust, political trust and non-institutionalised political participation in Western Europe. *West European Politics, 22*(3), 1–21.

Kang, X. (2002). Weilai 3–5 Nian Zhongguo Dalu zhengzhi wendingxing fenxi [Analyzing China's political stability in the three to five years ahead]. *Zhanlue Yu Guanli [Strategies and Management]* (3), 1–15.

Klingemann, H.-D. (1999). Mapping political support in the 1990s: A global analysis. In P. Norris (Ed.), *Critical citizens* (pp. 31–56). Oxford, United Kingdom: Oxford University Press.

Klingemann, H.-D. (2004). Support of democracy and confidence in government: On the ability of citizens to make distinctions. *Paper presented at "Citizens, Democracy and Markets around the Pacific Rim", March 19–20, 2004, The East–West Center, Honolulu, Hawaii.*

Kuh, G. D. (1991). *Involving colleges: Successful approaches to fostering student learning and development outside the classroom*. San Francisco: Jossey–Bass Publishers.

Li, L. (2004). Political trust in rural China. *Modern China, 30*(2), 228–258.

Linz, J. J., & Stepan, A. C. (1996). *Problems of democratic transition and consolidation: Southern Europe, South America, and post-communist Europe*. Baltimore: The Johns Hopkins University Press.

Lipset, S. M. (1960). *Political man: The social bases of politics*. Garden City, NY: Doubleday.

Liu, G. (1998). *Civic education in China: Past, present, and future challenges*. Yantai, China: Yantai Teacher's College.

Liu, M., & Ansfield, J. (2007, October 15). New crop of leaders could radically alter China. *Newsweek*.

Lovell, D. W. (2001). Trust and the politics of post-communism. *Communist and Post-Communist Studies, 34*(1), 27–38.

Lu, X. (2001). *Dangdai Zhongguo shehui jieceng yanjiu baogao [A study report of social stratification in contemporary China]*. Beijing: Zhongguo sheke wenxuan chubanshe.

Lynch, D. C. (1999). *After the propaganda state: Media, politics, and "thought work" in reformed China*. Stanford, CA: Stanford University Press.

Mcallister, I. (1999). The economic performance of governments. In P. Norris (Ed.), *Critical citizens* (pp. 169–187). Oxford, UK: Oxford University Press.

McFaul, M. (2002). The Fourth Wave of democracy and dictatorship: Noncooperative transitions in the Postcommunist world. *World Politics, 54*(2), 212–244.

Miller, A. H., Goldenberg, E. N., & Erbring, L. (1979). Type-set politics: Impact of newspapers on public confidence. *American Political Science Review, 73*(1), 67–84.

Mishler, W., & Rose, R. (1996). Trajectories of fear and hope: Support for democracy in post-communist Europe. *Comparative Political Studies, 28*, 553–581.

Mishler, W., & Rose, R. (1997). Trust, distrust and skepticism: Popular evaluations of civil and political institutions in Post-Communist societies. *Journal of Politics, 59*, 418–451.

Misztal, B. A. (1996). *Trust in modern societies: The search for the bases of social order*. Cambridge, UK: Polity Press.

Nathan, A. J. (1985). *Chinese democracy*. Berkeley: University of California Press.

Nathan, A. J. (2003). Authoritarian resilience. *Journal of Democracy, 14*(1), 6–17.

Nathan, A. J., & Ho, H. V. S. (1993). Chiang Ching-kuo's decision for political reform. In S.-C. Leng (Ed.), *Chiang Ching-kuo's leadership in the development of the Republic of China on Taiwan* (pp. 31–61). Lanham, MD: University Press of America.

Newton, K. (2001). Trust, social capital, civil society, and democracy. *International Political Science Review, 22*(2), 201–214.

Nie, N. H., Junn, J., & Stehlik-Barry, K. (1996). *Education and democratic citizenship in America*. Chicago: University of Chicago Press.

Norris, P. (1999a). *Critical citizens: Global support for democratic government*. New York: Oxford University Press.

Norris, P. (1999b). Introduction: The growth of critical citizens? In P. Norris (Ed.), *Critical Citizens* (pp. 1–27). Oxford, United Kingdom: Oxford University Press.

Norris, P. (2002). *Democratic phoenix: Reinventing political activism*. Cambridge, UK: Cambridge University Press.

Norris, P., & Inglehart, R. (2003). Islamic culture and democracy: Testing the "Clash of Civilizations" thesis. In R. Inglehart (Ed.), *Human values and social change: Findings from the World Values Surveys* (pp. 5–34): Brill.

O'Donnell, G., Schmitter, P. C., & Whitehead, L. (Eds.). (1986). *Transitions from authoritarian rule: Prospect for democracy*. Baltimore: The Johns Hopkins University Press.

Oh, J. K.-c. (1999). *Korean politics: The quest for democratization and economic development*. Ithaca, NY: Cornell University Press.

Ottaway, M. (2002). *Democracy challenged: The rise of semi-authoritarianism*. Washington, DC: Carnegie Endowment for International Peace.

Park, C.-M., & Shin, D. C. (2006). Do Asian values deter popular support for democracy in South Korea? *Asian Survey, 46*(3), 341–361.

Pascarella, E. T., & Terenzini, P. T. (1991). *How college affects students: Findings and insights from twenty years of research*. San Francisco: Jossey–Bass Publishers.

Pei, M. (2002). China's governance crisis. *Foreign Affairs, 81*(5), 96–119.

Pei, M. (2006). *China's trapped transition: The limits of developmental autocracy*. Cambridge, MA: Harvard University Press.

Pharr, S. J., & Putnam, R. D. (Eds.). (2000). *Disaffected democracies: What's troubling the trilateral countries?* Princeton, NJ: Princeton University Press.

Pharr, S. J., Putnam, R. D., & Dalton, R. J. (2000). A quarter century of declining confidence. *Journal of Democracy, 11*(2), 5–25.

Pridham, G. (2000). *The dynamics of democratization: A comparative approach*. London; New York: Continuum.

Przeworski, A., Alvarez, M. E., Cheibub, J. A., & Limongi, F. (2000). *Democracy and development: Political institutions and material well-being in the world, 1950–1990*. Cambridge: Cambridge University Press.

Przeworski, A., & Limongi, F. (1997). Modernization: Theories and facts. *World Politics, 49*(2), 155–183.

Putnam, R. D. (1993). *Making democracy work: Civic traditions in modern Italy*. Princeton, NJ: Princeton University Press.

Putnam, R. D. (1995). Bowling alone: America's declining social capital. *Journal of Democracy, 6*(1), 65–78.

Putnam, R. D. (2000). *Bowling alone: The collapse and revival of American community*. New York: Simon & Schuster.

Pye, L. W. (1968). *The spirit of Chinese politics: A psychocultural study of the authority crisis in political development*. Cambridge: M.I.T. Press.

Robinson, M. J. (1976). Public affairs television and the growth of political malaise: The case of "The Selling of the Pentagon." *American Political Science Review, 70*(2), 409–432.

Rose, R. (1994). Postcommunism and the problem of trust. *Journal of Democracy, 5*, 18–30.

Rose, R. (2002). How Muslims views democracy: Evidence from Central Asia. *Journal of Democracy, 13*(4), 102–111.

Rose, R., & Shin, D. C. (2001). Democratization backwards: The problem of Third-Wave democracies. *British Journal of Political Science, 31*, 331–354.

Ross, M. L. (2001). Does oil hinder democracy? *World Politics, 53*(3), 325–361.

Rossabi, M. (1992). Mongolia: A new opening? *Current History, 91*(566), 278–283.

Rowen, H. S. (1995). The tide underneath the "Third Wave." *Journal of Democracy, 6*(1), 52–64.

Rowen, H. S. (2007). When will the Chinese people be free? *Journal of Democracy, 18*(3), 38–52.

Schaffer, F. C. (1998). *Democracy in translation*. Ithaca, NY: Cornell University Press.

Schoem, D. L., & Hurtado, S. (2001). *Intergroup dialogue: Deliberative democracy in school, college, community, and workplace*. Ann Arbor: University of Michigan Press.

Scott, J. C. (1985). *Weapons of the weak: Everyday forms of peasant resistance*. New Haven, CT: Yale University Press.

Sen, A. (1999). *Development as freedom*. New York: Alfred Knopf.

Shin, D. C., & Park, C.-M. (2003). *The democratization of mass political orientations in South Korea: Ascertaining the cultural dimension of democratic consolidation*. Unpublished manuscript, Columbia, MO.

Song, Y.-B. (2002, Jan, 22). *Crisis of cultural identity in East Asia: On the meaning of Confucian ethics in the age of globalization.* Paper presented at the University of Michigan Center for Chinese Studies Lecture Series, Ann Arbor.

Tarrow, S. G. (1998). *Power in movement: Social movements and contentious politics* (2nd ed.). Cambridge; New York: Cambridge University Press.

Temple, J. (1999). The new growth evidence. *Journal of Economic Literature, 37*, 112–156.

Tessler, M. (2002). Do Islamic orientations influence attitudes toward democracy in the Arab World? Evidence from Egypt, Jordan, Morocco, and Algeria. *International Journal of Comparative Sociology, 43*(3/5), 229–249.

Tu, W.-M. (2000a). Implications of the rise of "Confucian" East Asia. *Daedalus, 129*(1), 195–218.

Tu, W.-M. (2000b). Multiple modernities: A preliminary inquiry into the implications of East Asian modernity. In L. E. Harrison & S. P. Huntington (Eds.), *Culture matters: How values shape human progress* (pp. 256–267). New York: Basic Books.

Vanhanen, T. (1997). *Prospects of democracy: A study of 172 countries*. London; New York: Routledge.

Varshney, A. (2002). *Ethnic conflict and civic life: Hindus and Muslims in India*. New Haven, CT: Yale University Press.

Verba, S., Nie, N. H., & Kim, J.-o. (1978). *Participation and political equality: A seven-nation comparison*. New York: Cambridge University Press.

Wang, S. (2003). The problem of state weakness. *Journal of Democracy, 14*(1), 36–42.

Wang, Z. (2007). Public support for democracy in China. *Journal of Contemporary China, 16*(53), 561–579.

Warren, M. E. (Ed.). (2004). *Democracy and trust*. Cambridge, UK: Cambridge University Press

Welzel, C. (2006). Democratization as an emancipative process: The neglected role of mass motivations. *European Journal of Political Research, 45*(6), 871–896.

Welzel, C., & Inglehart, R. (2005). Democratization as the growth of freedom: The human development perspective. *Japanese Journal of Political Science 6*(3), 313–343.

Welzel, C., Inglehart, R., & Deutsch, F. (2005). Social capital, voluntary associations and collective action: Which aspects of social capital have the greatest 'civic' payoff? *Journal of Civil Society, 1*(2), 121–146

Welzel, C., Inglehart, R., & Klingemann, H.-D. (2003). The theory of human development: A cross-cultural analysis. *European Journal of Political Research, 42*(2), 341–379.

Wright, T. (2001). *The perils of protest: State repression and student activism in China and Taiwan*. Honolulu: University of Hawai'i Press.

Yang, D. (2004). *Remaking the Chinese Leviathan: Market transition and the politics of governance in China*. Stanford, CA: Stanford University Press.

Yang, D. (2007). China's long march to freedom. *Journal of Democracy, 18*(3), 58–64.

Yu, J. (2003). Nongmin youzuzhi kangzheng ji qi zhengzhi fengxian [Organized resistances of peasants and their political risks]. *Zhanlue yu Guanli [Strategies and Management]* (3), 1–16.

Zabaria, F. (1994). Culture is destiny: A conversation with Lee Kuan Yew. *Foreign Affairs, 73*(2), 109–126.

Zha, J. (1995). *China pop: How soap operas, tabloids, and bestsellers are transforming a culture*. New York: New Press; Distributed by W.W. Norton.

Zhao, D. (2000). *The power of Tiananmen*. Chicago: University of Chicago Press.

Zheng, Y. (2004). *Will China become democratic? Elite, class and regime transition*. Singapore: East Asia Institute.

Index

www.ingramcontent.com/pod-product-compliance
Ingram Content Group UK Ltd.
Pitfield, Milton Keynes, MK11 3LW, UK
UKHW041121071026
15587UKWH00009B/22

9 781934 043998